HOW TO WRITE LIKE A PROFESSIONAL

HOW TO WRITE LIKE A PROFESSIONAL

J.L. Barkas, Ph.D.

ARCO PUBLISHING, INC.
New York

Published by Arco Publishing, Inc.
215 Park Avenue South, New York, N.Y. 10003

Library of Congress Cataloging in Publication Data

Barkas, J. L. (Janet L.)
  How to write like a professional.

  Includes index.
  1. Authorship. I. Arco Publishing. II. Title.
PN147.B3236   1985   808'.02   84-18619
ISBN 0-668-05676-2 (Cloth Edition)
ISBN 0-668-05680-0 (Paper Edition)

Printed in the United States of America

For my sister Eileen

Contents

Acknowledgments   ix
Preface   xi

1 Words, Words, Words: An Introduction   1
2 Writer's Block   11
3 Tools of the Trade   31
4 Content   45
5 Style   69
6 Writing for Work, School, or Personal Reasons   87
7 Getting Your Writing Published   103
8 Conclusion: Building on the Skills You Have   137

Index   159

Acknowledgments

I want to thank teachers, editors, publishers, and fellow writers for their help over the years, especially Beatrice Salzman, Hayes B. Jacobs, Nancy Creshkoff, Nona Aguilar, George Ehrlich, Sidney Offit, and members of the American Society of Journalists and Authors (ASJA). Not to be ignored are those whom I have interviewed, or who filled out my questionnaires, for this book on writing, including those colleagues, such as Howard Rebach and Roland Wingfield, who took the time to comment on drafts of chapters or sections of this manuscript.

Preface

Are you intimidated when your boss asks you to have a report ready by next Friday? Would you like to write a publishable letter to the editor? Are your memos readable? Do you procrastinate about writing assignments, even if you want to do them? Have you always wanted to write like a professional? This book is for everyone who would like to write, but is afraid, or who would like to write better, but does not know how. This is, in fact, the book I could have used when I was a student, then an executive secretary, an editor, and a budding professional nonfiction writer. It is my hope that this book will help you master nonfiction (or "expository") writing by providing you with an understanding of the basics of good writing. Whether you write because you have to, or because you want to; whether you never earn anything from your writing; or whether it someday makes you rich, effective writing can help you to become more successful and more self-aware.

There are scores of books for would-be and professional writers, scholars, and social scientists, and for those who wish to improve their grammar or style. This book brings together the basics of style and content in one compact and readable volume. It is not intended to replace or substitute for more detailed guides to grammar or research. Instead, this book is intended as a starting point for those who feel inadequate as nonfiction writers, or as a refresher for those who want a new outlook on their craft. To facilitate your reading, I am omitting footnotes, although references are given throughout the text and in bibliographies at the end of each chapter. If you want to study any of the topics in this book, such as library research, word processors, libel, grammar, business-letter writing, or getting published, more intensively, you will find supplementary sources listed in the bibliographies.

I hope that you enjoy reading this book and doing the writing exercises that conclude each chapter. There are, basically, two paths to writing better:

Write more.
Read more.

"Writing more" goes beyond the exercises in this book to the business or personal writing projects that you have to do, or that you are contemplating. "Reading more" means exposing yourself to good writing, by classic authors of the past and by exemplary contemporary writers. Biographer and critic André Maurois expressed how reading aids writing in *The Art of Writing* (New York: Dutton, 1960), giving sound advice regardless of a writer's age:

> The best training for the young writer is to be found in a reading of the masters. A close study of them will show him how a masterpiece is made. Familiarity with the methods of the great will provide him with great examples. At first he will read for pleasure, like any young enthusiast with a taste for books. Then, having become familiar with this or that work, he will return to it again and again with the purpose of "taking it to pieces" and seeing just how its effects are obtained.

In this book I share with you my own hard-won knowledge of writing so that you can gain the confidence and pleasure in nonfiction writing that I took some fifteen years to achieve. I have seven nonfiction books, one dissertation, one thesis, and dozens of newspaper, journal, and magazine articles to my credit since my first article appeared in a national magazine in 1972, so I think I can provide you with insights and tips that will enable *you* to write more easily and more confidently. You can free yourself from the fears and myths about writing that inhibit you. Nonfiction writing can be an exhilarating experience; it is surely a necessary skill.

1

Words, Words, Words: An Introduction

Good nonfiction writing is a powerful tool for advancement in all careers and personal endeavors. What exactly is nonfiction writing? A memo, a speech, a term paper, a postcard to a relative, and a magazine article are just a few examples. "Nonfiction" is factual writing that instructs, persuades, or amuses. Also called expository writing or prose, nonfiction is basically all writing that is not novels, short stories, plays, poetry, or screenplays.

Writing effectively is both an art and a skill. A certain amount of talent enhances nonfiction writing. However, to write well you need not be a literary genius. Clear and thoughtful prose will take you quite far.

This book is based on my experiences as an editor, a writing teacher, and a published nonfiction writer. To research this book, and to augment my own writing and editing experiences, I have collected 165 three-page questionnaires from professional and occasional writers, including business managers, executives, and students, and conducted dozens of telephone and in-person interviews with writers, would-be writers, and teachers of writing. My experiences in teaching nonfiction writing at Pennsylvania State University were a principal inspiration for this book. I discovered early that few of my students intended to become professional writers. Most students just wanted to learn basic nonfiction writing techniques to aid them in job hunting or long-term career advancement, or to use writing as a means of self-expression. After a careful reading of writing assignments, I realized almost all the students needed help with the basics of nonfiction writing (content and style) and with acquiring a fresh outlook on expository writing. For example, the idea of rewriting their assignments once or twice, let alone five or six times, was anathema to most. They considered writing as equivalent to speaking—whatever came out the first time was what was submitted as the final product. But the beauty of writing is that you *do* get a second, a third, or as many chances as needed to make your words more closely match your thoughts.

Nonfiction writing is a unique skill in that *everyone* has to do it, professional or not. Consider: Unless you are a composer, your employer will not ask you to write a song. Unless you are an artist, your teacher will not base your grade on your prowess at painting. However, almost all employers and teachers ask you to write a report or to take essay exams. You will have to write at your job, at school, or in carrying out your personal affairs, and if you do not write well, it *will* be held against you.

"You can't teach someone how to write," a high school English teacher recently warned me. I protested. "Someone can write or he can't," she persisted. I thought of a nonfiction writing teacher who echoed her sentiments. In this teacher's view, one student had "it." Another student did not. Today, the first student runs a real estate business. The second student continues to write and to be published. Dr. Terence Moran, who has taught writing in public high schools and is now a faculty member in the Department of Communication Arts and Sciences at New York University, believes writing *can* be taught. Professor Moran explains:

> I've taught writing for a number of years and I think I can get students to write. . . . I try to convince my students that they have something to say. Once they realize they *do* have something to say, they can write. I found that if you provide a structure, you can get anybody to write. You can get people to frame their ideas in the right way. You don't make them all best-selling novelists, but you can make anyone a better writer by focusing on the process of writing. It's revision writing. You write as a process, not as a product. Good writers usually strike a balance between revising and completion. In the past it used to be taught that writing was either good or bad. Either your [writing] piece made it into a literary magazine, or it didn't. No one questioned *why* you were doing something. Now we teach writing as something that is *process* oriented.

In the next chapter you'll learn what's behind the myth that many still believe about nonfiction writing, namely that "Writers are born, not made." For now, applaud yourself for dispelling that myth by deciding to read this book, to do its exercises, and to learn more about the craft of nonfiction writing.

In *On Writing Well*, William Zinsser states that the "heart of good nonfiction writing" is "humanity and warmth." Veteran journalist Theodore Irwin writes in *Writing the Magazine Article* (Ed. Beatrice Schapper; Cincinnati: Writer's Digest, 1970) that his nonfiction writing is driven by another force: "Convinced that an idea is sound, I don't give up." If you're not yet a seasoned pro like Irwin, however, developing an idea into a finished manuscript may involve learning a lot more than just perseverance. Irwin, and successful nonfiction writers like him, are dedicated researchers and superb craftsmen with words. They are able and willing to write, edit, revise, and rewrite again, as necessary.

What distinguishes competent nonfiction writers? Knowledge helps. Patience facilitates revising and rewriting. A way with words is useful. Wit may make you a star. Yet absence of any or all of the above traits does not rule out competent nonfiction writing. It is *self-confidence* that is imperative for the nonfiction writer. A dearth of self-confidence inhibits committing ideas to paper.

How does a nonfiction writer develop the necessary self-confidence to write effectively? In writing, as in anything else, self-confidence comes from competence. Competence in nonfiction writing comes from following these four basic steps:

1. Know what you want to say.
2. Identify your audience.
3. Organize your thoughts.
4. Write and rewrite.

This process is neither a mysterious nor a magical one. Self-confidence follows once you know what you want to say (your content), and how you're going to write it (your style). A nonfiction writer perfects skills by practicing: writing, rewriting, researching, rewriting, editing, and rewriting.

Achieving greater competence in your nonfiction writing will certainly make the process of writing more palatable. Interest wanes if there is little positive reinforcement for your efforts. Bowling gets too frustrating if your score never improves; tennis becomes tedious if you rarely get the ball over the net. Learning the basics of nonfiction writing improves the possibility that your written words will more closely match the ideas that you intend to convey.

Let's expand your concept of nonfiction writing from a general idea into a seven-step process:

1. Decide on your topic: what you want to (or have to) write about.
2. Gather your facts: Research any preliminary or additional information that you will need to complete the writing project/assignment.
3. Organize your information: Make a road map that you will follow (a list of points to be covered or a detailed outline).
4. Write a first draft.
5. Revise as needed.
6. Submit your writing.
7. Integrate criticisms of this writing, if and when appropriate to do so (e.g., rewrite this material or apply those criticisms to current or future writings).

These seven steps are interdependent; a direct line from #1 to #7 rarely occurs. You may need to start with Step 2, for example, if your topic evolves from your research. You might find that Step 4 causes you to come up with a completely different Step 1, and you'll then start the process all over again. You might wish to write a first draft based on what you already know and then do research to fill in the gaps. Perhaps you will want to apply Step 7 to every draft you write rather than waiting until your final one. More important, each type of nonfiction writing that you do—memo, report, magazine article, or book—will require emphasizing certain steps and deemphasizing others.

Those who write nonfiction effectively have certain common traits. They strive to achieve facility in writing. They support their ideas with facts and examples gleaned from their own lives or through research. They are curious about people, places, and things. They are probing individuals who want to find out "why" and "how." They read good writing. They practice writing. They value critical evaluation of their work (rather than treat it as a judgment about them personally). You may find it interesting that some professional writers dislike the actual act of writing. They (like you, perhaps) prefer to "have written." One seasoned book author, for example, finds the planning stage of his writing projects the most enjoyable part and rewriting his various drafts the least palatable. A disciplined man, however, aware of the pitfalls of giving into writer's block, he does not allow himself to avoid writing tasks for longer than a few days.

Writer's block, the temporary or prolonged inability to put words on paper, can have dire personal and professional consequences. Unless you have unlimited access to a Wats line, communicating by phone, especially long distance, is becoming too expensive. Most jobs require proficient writing skills. Blanking out on an exam, a form of writer's block, can hamper school performance. In order to achieve the rewards of nonfiction writing, pros and occasional writers alike have to go beyond what they enjoy or dislike about writing so that the written product becomes a reality. If you let a distaste for isolation or rewriting stop you from writing, you will prevent yourself from enjoying its benefits. For all nonfiction writers, seasoned pros or novices, it is the final product that counts. This book will provide you with ways to become more relaxed about, and competent with, the writing process, so that you will write more often, and better, than before.

Before your formal education ends, you may have little or inadequate exposure to the techniques that will help you to improve your nonfiction writing. High school and college composition classes are worthwhile, as far as they go. Graduate programs that train scholars in specialized fields and that are supposed to help their students to fulfill a lifetime mandate to publish may not include even a single writing course in their four- or five-year programs. An executive whom I interviewed is proud that his company provides intensive training in nonfiction writing for its employees. I asked how long that program lasts. "One full workday," he answered. That's a start, to be sure, and one- and two-day writing workshops for managers and executives get results. However, if you want to reap the personal and professional benefits of better written communication, you will have to continue to practice and to improve your writing on your own. The assumption is: You can read, can't you? Then why aren't you able to write lucid prose?

Charles Kaiser, the articulate president of Pannell Kerr Forster, a national accounting firm, shares his observations about how poor writing inhibits an accountant's career advancement:

> Eventually the person who is writing bad letters will look for a new job because he or she will not have the advancement that he or she might expect. Technical competency for an accountant—a good understanding of accounting principles, auditing standards, tax laws, and the ability to communicate—are the *minimum* requirements for career advancement. . . . At a [certain] point, you *have* to be able to write well. . . . Therefore, if you write poorly, you look stupid. The audit report, the management report, the letter of transmittal to a tax return are forms of communication. An audit report isn't numbers. If you have an improperly written footnote, it detracts [from the report]. Misspelling or using a plural verb with a singular subject detracts from the body of knowledge you're trying to convey.

These comments are applicable to most jobs. Just how devastating a poorly written memo can be to a career is highlighted in this remark quoted in Priscilla Vail's *Clear and Lively Writing* (New York: Walker & Co., 1981): " 'I got a memo the other day, and after I had read it, I didn't know whether I was supposed to congratulate the guy on a triumph or fire him for incompetence.' "

Why do *you* want to improve your nonfiction writing? Having clear objectives will provide reinforcement as you read this book and do the practical writing exercises that conclude each chapter. Take a moment to ponder your reasons for wanting to write better. Is your insecurity about your writing stifling your professional or personal growth? Do you have a gnawing feeling that there are ideas you would put down on paper if you just knew how? Think for a few minutes—or longer. Then fill in the self-evaluation that follows and date it. Buy yourself a notebook and begin a daily nonfiction writing journal. Copy your answers into your journal as your first entry. More will be said about keeping a journal in subsequent chapters. For now, consider your journal a way of keeping track of your ideas, your feelings about writing, research notes, and so forth.

Reasons for Improving My Nonfiction Writing

Date: _____

1. _____
2. _____
3. _____
4. _____

Consider the effectiveness of your current writing style and in what ways you want to improve it. Take the nonfiction writing self-evaluation that follows. The evaluation reflects some basic writing concerns, as noted in such classic books about writing as Strunk and White's *The Elements of Style* and Flesch's *How to Say What You Mean in Plain English.* Use this self-evaluation to create a beginning point for your self-study program of improving the style of your writing. Considering these evaluation questions and the guidelines that follow them will help you to begin recognizing the elements of good writing.

Writing Style Self-Evaluation

Date: _____

	Yes	No
1. Do you write with ease or agony?	—	—
2. Do you check your spelling against the dictionary?	✓	—
3. Is your writing clear?	—	✓
4. Do you use flowery language?	✓	—
5. Do you use thousands, nay, millions of commas?	✓	—
6. Do you gear your writing to a specific audience?	✓	—
7. Do you create an outline (or make a list of points to cover) before you write?	—	✓
8. Are you open to criticisms of your writing?	✓	—
9. Do you read good writers?	✓	—
10. Are you self-confident about your writing?	✓	—

The statements that follow in response to the questions will help you to assess some of your current writing problems. If with the help of this book you can achieve these basic goals, you will become a better writer:

1. Make your writing flow as naturally as your speech.
2. Check and correct your spelling, unless you want to appear illiterate.
3. Always strive for clarity.
4. Avoid flowery or fancy words.
5. Use commas where necessary, and only where necessary. Take the time to master correct punctuation. Poorly punctuated writing is unclear.
6. Allow your specific audience to determine not only *what* you write but *how* you write it.
7. Organize your writing by using outlines or lists of points to be covered, especially for longer or more complicated writing tasks.
8. Attempt to handle criticism of your writing constructively: This will enable you to improve your skills.
9. Improve your writing by writing more and reading more. If you read junk, you'll write junk.
10. Try to improve the reliability (content) and readability (style) of your writing. Your self-confidence will increase as you become more competent.

Don't get discouraged if your answers to the self-evaluation displease you. You will find information, examples, and exercises throughout this book to help you correct these and other common writing problems. Chapter 2, for example, will explore writer's block, a major obstacle to writing well (or writing at all). Chapter 3 will highlight the tools and resources that might help you to write more easily. Chapter 4 will discuss *what* you want to say—the content of your writing. Chapter 5 will look at *how* you're going to say it—the style or readability of your writing. Chapter 6 will show how to apply your improved nonfiction writing skills to business, school, or personal use. Chapter 7 describes how to get your writing published in a variety of markets (newspapers, magazines, journals, books, etc.). Chapter 8 offers additional resources for building on your nonfiction writing skills, including the development of a writing plan, as well as participation in conferences and organizations that might aid you in becoming a more effective communicator in writing.

A few words about the exercises and suggested readings at the end of each chapter. Do as many exercises as you can. You learn to write by writing, and practice helps. No one will slap your hands or embarrass you if your writing is weak or incorrect. These exercises are for *you*. If possible, however, show your writing exercises to people whose opinions you value. Learn to benefit from their reactions and suggestions.

EXERCISES

1. What is good writing? Write down two or three sentences that summarize anything you have thus far learned about writing effectively. (Record your answers in your daily writing journal.)

2. List three nonfiction writing projects you want to (or have to) start, work on, or complete:

   1._____
   2._____
   3._____

   Do you have a deadline for one or all of these projects? If not, decide on a realistic deadline that you will try to meet. Transfer this information into your daily writing journal and onto a master calendar. (For longer writing tasks, begin to consider how each writing task could be broken up into steps, each step with a specific deadline.)

3. Do you have one or more favorite nonfiction writers? Exposure to good writing will provide you with examples for improving your own writing. Pick one book, author, or magazine that you will read critically. Note where the writing grabs you, loses your interest, educates you, makes a point in an original and memorable way, how it ends, etc. Some contemporary nonfiction writers you might want to read include: Isaac Asimov, Russell Baker, Studs Terkel, Tom Wolfe, Alvin Toffler, Joan Didion, Berton Roueche, James Michener, Erica Jong, and Martin Mayer.

4. Set aside an hour each day that you will devote to writing. If you don't have any pressing writing projects right

now, use that time to write in your nonfiction journal, or to redo (rewrite) any writing exercises in this book.

REFERENCES

Elbow, Peter. *Writing With Power.* New York: Oxford University Press, 1981. Based on Elbow's experiences as a college writing teacher, this is a thorough and useful self-study guide for expository writing. Most chapters are summarized with helpful key writing tips.

Flesch, Rudolf. *How to Say What You Mean in Plain English.* New York: Barnes & Noble Books, 1972. A classic guide, laden with examples, of how to write as clearly as you speak.

Schapper, Beatrice, ed. *Writing the Magazine Article: From Idea to Printed Page.* Cincinnati: Writer's Digest, 1970. Eight members of the Society of Magazine Writers (now called the American Society of Journalists and Authors) share the genesis of specific articles, including getting the assignment, doing the research, writing and rewriting, and getting the piece accepted. The exhibits of manuscript pages in this excellent collection graphically demonstrate that even for professional writers, writing is *rewriting.*

Strunk, William, Jr., and E.B. White. *The Elements of Style,* 2nd ed. New York: Macmillan, 1972. Rules for clear, effective writing, along with excellent examples, make this seventy-eight-page book necessary reading for all nonfiction writers.

Zinsser, William. *On Writing Well,* 2nd ed. New York: Harper & Row, 1980. Developed from the nonfiction writing course that Zinsser taught at Yale, this book discusses eighteen important areas, including simplicity, style, the audience, the lead, writing in your job, criticism, and humor.

2

Writer's Block

I just couldn't take looking at that blank sheet a moment
longer. . . . So I tore it up. I just couldn't take it.

—Anonymous

Professional and occasional writers alike may experience
writer's block. The results of writer's block are those blank pages
our anonymous friend referred to above. These pages may wind
up crumpled on the floor amid others, or filled with discarded
words. The net result is no useful words.

I should confess at once that I am certainly not immune to
writer's block. At one point while I was supposed to be writing
this book, I spent two weeks reorganizing my clothing. I rear-
ranged condiments and books. I even got inside my filing cabinets, unearthing all manner of pungent memorabilia. My block
miraculously disappeared when an editor told me that if I did not
have the manuscript ready on time, dire results would ensue.
Deadlines may, indeed, dispel a writer's block—or they may
plunge one even further into the depths of literary fright. It is also
true that some writing projects, perhaps even the ones that will
advance you the furthest, are those tasks you set out to do on your
own, with self-imposed deadlines that are no less real than those
imposed by others.

Procrastination is the most blatant symptom of writer's
block. Writing is delayed. It may be put off for hours, weeks,
years, or indefinitely. Its less obvious symptoms are panic, ambiv-
alence, fear, anger, or compulsive behavior. Writer's block may
be operating when words are set down in a strained way. In *Overcoming Writing Blocks,* authors Karin Mack and Eric Skjei explain: "A writing block is, quite simply, an obstacle to the free
expression of ideas on paper. Somewhere between the thought
and the recording of it there is an interruption in the flow."

In its most severe form, having writer's block means that writing is avoided completely. Reports are not written. Business letters are left unanswered. Dissertations are abandoned. In milder forms, writing occurs in spurts. Those sporadic periods of writing may be pleasurable or excruciating. Between spurts, the blocked writer agonizes. Some raid the ice box. Some talk on the phone. Some make paper airplanes. Some spend more time staring than writing. Writer's block may mean an inability to start, to keep writing, to "find the right words," or to finish.

A professional writer would have to switch careers if a temporary block became permanent. The consequences of blocking may be more subtle for the nonprofessional writer. Sadly, activities that replace the delayed writing are tinged by a feeling of failure. Joan, thirty-four, a graduate student who has had writer's block for more than a year, says: "Substituting another activity, even one with redeeming social value, for the writing task one *should* be doing robs that substitute activity of the full satisfaction or pleasure that it would otherwise provide." Nancy, thirty-nine, a researcher at a corporation, sometimes blocks when she has to write a business memo. Nancy explains what those writing blocks are like:

> I know I have writer's block when I find I'm stalling, procrastinating, staring at a blank sheet of paper for an unusual period of time, making phone calls, rereading the material about which I'm writing the memo but not succeeding in putting anything down on paper, and coming close to a deadline and starting to feel anxious that I'm not going to meet it. Those memos that I don't block on are probably a little bit better and easier. I've never suffered writer's block because I'm bored. If I suffer writer's block it's because I just can't figure out *how* I want to say what I want to say or I can't figure out *what* I want to say. Writer's block to me is the desire [to write] but, for some reason, the inability to do so. Ultimately the memo gets written. . . . [But] writer's block is not very pleasant.

Although Nancy's memos eventually get done, for others, blocking on one writing task may develop into a general writer's block. It may take years to realize how writer's block inhibits a successful nonwriting career. Brian, thirty-four, an assistant professor at an eastern college, does not have to write for a living. His academic status, however, might be advanced if he could manage to write and publish even one article a year. Brian describes the writer's block that has plagued him in the six years since he finished his dissertation:

What about the inability to write at all? I can come up with great ideas. I can come up with them in my head. I can even sketch them out on paper. I've never written them out. I've never gotten beyond the point of having these great ideas. I had an idea recently and I don't know if I'll follow it through. . . . I sketched out in my head how I would do this. Great idea. That's as far as it's gotten. I've never sat down and gotten anywhere in terms of writing out an outline, in terms of pursuing possible funding for it, [in terms of] writing to anyone about it.

What I do when I have a writer's block is come up with another idea. . . . I don't even get as far as the typewriter. I find something else to do. Another excuse. I have to prepare for classes. I don't turn the interest into action. I've never had a deadline. I've never created a deadline for myself. I've never done that kind of thing. My dissertation took me seven years. Two of those years it sat on the shelf and collected dust. There's a two-year hiatus in there when literally nothing got done. . . . Part of the writer's block was to have the notion in my mind to do this great piece of work, earth shattering, and of course nothing I ever put down on paper ever came close to the image of that. I was supposed to change intellectual history. There was implicit encouragement at my graduate school to think along the lines of the great piece of work. . . .

Professionally, writing would give me recognition, advancement, getting myself a track record that I could then use to get other kinds of professional opportunities, like lecturing, consulting, or other writing jobs. Professionally, it [writing] would help me to do some of the things I feel comfortable doing. I like to do research [for example].

In my survey of professional and occasional writers, 75 percent experienced writer's block; 25 percent never did. Experiencing writer's block had nothing to do with whether someone was a full-time professional writer; those who wrote an occasional memo were as likely to experience it as those who wrote a book a year. Writer's block seems to be a question of personality; either you are the kind of person who blocks or you're not. For those who do, 56 percent have a pattern to their blocks (34 percent do not have a pattern and 10 percent did not answer that question). Of those experiencing writer's block, only 18 percent cannot write at all during the period of the block, or think of giving up writing. For the 75 percent who experience writer's block, the most frequent manifestations or causes of their blocks,* in order of frequency, are:

- Inability to find the right words (34 percent)
- Feeling upset and anxious (34 percent)
- Belief that writer's block is tied to the writer's moods (30 percent)
- "I don't know what causes it." (14 percent)
- Inability to get started (13 percent)
- Tied to a particular kind of writing (6 percent)
- Failure of writing or thinking to flow (5 percent)
- Disorganized material (4 percent)
- Burnout (3 percent)
- Fear of criticism (3 percent)
- Lack of self-confidence (2 percent)
- Trying something more difficult than usual (2 percent)
- Deadline pressure (1 percent)

I'm sharing these writing survey results to give you concrete evidence that if you experience writer's block, you are in the majority. Writer's block has nothing to do with whether you are an occasional, part-time, or full-time professional writer. There are, of course, some people who are immune to writer's block; you will certainly block less as you gain confidence in your writing. Ted, forty-three, a prolific reviewer and columnist, for example, never blocks: "Writer's block is a mystery to me because I have never encountered it. My problem is tearing myself away from the typewriter." However, those of us who sometimes find it hard to *get* to the typewriter, or, once there, to make words flow, should not despair. *Experiencing* writer's block is not a problem.

---

* Percentages total more than 100 percent because respondents checked or filled in one to seven answers. The majority provided one answer (40 percent) or two answers (26 percent); the rest provided zero, 3, 4, 5, or 7 responses. This analysis is based on 125 questionnaires from adult professional and occasional writers.

Journalists on the staff of major newspapers who completed my survey, for instance, did not let a block of one or even several hours prevent them from getting a story in on time. What does count, however, is whether you give in by giving up, whether the reason is that you do not feel like writing, you are frightened of outside criticism, you have difficulty finding the right words, you are bored, you are unable to get started after putting your writing aside for a while, and so forth. Writer's block is quite common; how long it lasts is up to you. A college professor who experiences occasional writer's block says this about her blocks:

> There are days when I simply *can't* write. There are days when I can't teach as well; the words just don't flow. This doesn't happen frequently, but it's easy to identify. I start leaving blanks when I can't think of *the* correct word. This phenomenon does not appear to be related to moods or how I feel physically. It just occurs. I jokingly liken it to the phases of the moon, or biorhythms.

Consider the difference in writer's block as experienced by the professional versus the sometime writer:

Professional writer's block: "I have to write, but I can't right now."

Sometime writer's block: "I don't want to write, and anyway, I can't."

To conquer writer's block, think about some myths about writing that may actually cause blocking.

MYTH 1: "WRITERS ARE BORN, NOT MADE"

Belief in this myth gets you off the hook. Writer's block confirms that writing well is inherited. As you will learn by reading this and other books on writing, *nonfiction writing is a skill that can be learned*. Nonfiction writing is hard work. *While a place in the literary hall of fame is not guaranteed, expressing ideas clearly is possible.*

MYTH 2: "I CAN'T WRITE UNLESS I GET THE URGE"

You are confusing perspiration with inspiration.

Be realistic about the urge that motivates the professional versus the sometime writer:

Professional writer's urge: "I don't know why, but I *have* to write."

Sometime writer's urge: "I don't want to, but I *have* to write."

Brian, the assistant professor, explains how by clinging to the "urge" theory of writing he has perpetuated his writer's block:

I thought writing was something almost like lust; it happened to you. When it happened to you, the words flowed out of you. I never thought writing was work. . . . So if it wasn't coming out I said, "Well, I'm not ready yet. The ideas aren't pouring out, I've got to think about it a bit more." So I always thought you had to be inspired to write. I never thought you had to be self-disciplined to write, so I never disciplined myself. . . . I sat around waiting for the bolt of lightning to come out of the blue to hit me in the head and suddenly for the pen to start, and it hasn't. It hasn't happened.

MYTH 3: "IT HAS TO COME OUT RIGHT THE FIRST TIME"

Although some professional writers are able to get their first draft accepted, most have to rewrite two, three, five, or more times. Writing means writing, editing, and rewriting. As one sometime writer says: "If you cannot bear to review, rewrite, and edit your own words at least a second or third time, how can you expect anyone else to want to read it even once?"

Psychologist-painter Desy Safán-Gerard infers that demanding that your writing be perfect the first time is self-indulgent. In "How to Unblock," an article that appeared in *Psychology Today*, Safán-Gerard writes: An "unwillingness to edit or change . . . does not really improve communication. . . ." Safán-Gerard continues, pointing out that placing such unrealistic demands on oneself may cause a block: "Trying to make work fit a preconceived idea often produces . . . a creative block." Thus, trying for perfection in your first draft may cause writer's block and may also adversely affect your writing if you get past the block. You might force your writing to fit your earliest ideas rather than let the act of writing reshape your views. This book is based on the premise that writing is a process; rewriting is part of that process. Some writers describe that process as an all-consuming, trancelike state; ideas emerge and are used or rejected. Words are considered, substituted, reconsidered, added, or deleted. This is a far cry from the preconceived notion of "getting it right the first time." Good writing is fluid, not static; effective writing contradicts the "right the first time" theory.

There is a place for perfectionism in nonfiction writing, but it should only rarely be your concern when you sit down to do the first draft. Perfectionism, or trying to make the best match between your ideas and your words, is beneficial during the editing, revising, and rewriting phases of nonfiction writing. Those who fail to write anything because they want it to be right the first time are like those who fail to write a book because they fear it will not be as brilliant as their fantasies. Instead of trying to write the best book they can, they write nothing at all.

MYTH 4: "I DON'T HAVE ENOUGH INFORMATION TO START WRITING"

Truman Capote began writing *In Cold Blood* some four years and six thousand pages of notes after he began his research. Carefully consider your own need to know. Are you delaying writing because of a genuine need for information, or because writing and rewriting are more tedious than conducting research? One sometime writer who gets writer's block because of a tendency to overresearch explains:

Now that I think back on a report I had to do I realize that I always seemed to get off on tangents. . . . It's happening again to me right now. I have a whole file in my office [related to my newest project] which I've never even had a chance to read. How can I write anything unless I read that stuff? The problem is, as soon as I read it, there will be twenty-five other things that I'll discover I haven't read. That will lead to fifty more things that I haven't read. How can I write anything if I haven't read everything written on the subject, or everything *possibly* written on the subject?

Consider putting down on paper what you already know. Use the writing process to highlight which facts are missing. You may be surprised to learn how much you have already discovered!

MYTH 5: "I NEED A LOT OF TIME ALONE TO WRITE"

Full-time professional writers have the hard-won luxury of hours of time alone to write. For others, compromises and adjustments must be made. Newspaper reporters learn to write in large, noisy rooms surrounded by dozens of other writers and editors. "You really just get used to doing it. There's just no option, no way of removing it," says *Newsday* reporter Drew Fetherston. "There's really no way of avoiding it. It's a condition of the workplace," Fetherston continues. Executives immune to this myth put a sign on their door to get even an hour of time alone to write. Housewives who are serious about writing wake up at five in the morning to find some time to themselves. If you live alone, make a study corner in the living room and work there after dinner. If you live with others, consider creating a study corner in any area that the rest of the family need not come into—convert a large closet, if necessary. Search out a nook that can be yours for a few hours, whether at home or at the office. Write for two or three hours over the weekend. Find an hour each morning or at night when you can write uninterrupted. Have your secretary answer your phone. Buy an answering machine to take your calls when you are working at home, or have a family member take messages for you. Go to the library if it is impossible to avoid home or office distractions. Check into a hotel room for a night, if necessary, to allow yourself to concentrate totally. However, less-than-ideal writing conditions are no excuse for a writer's block.

MYTH 6: "THEY WON'T LIKE WHAT I'VE WRITTEN"

They may not like what you've written, but they also may not like what you've said, and that doesn't stop you from talking, does it? Although pleasing your audience is an important consideration, you should not let the fear of displeasing an audience inhibit your writing. Turn your fear of outside criticism into healthy self-criticism that inspires you to rewrite until *you* are pleased. Carol Ann Finkelstein, a sociologist who has done an extensive study of women stockbrokers, explains how this theory promotes writer's block:

> The whole notion of the fear of failure, fear of evaluation, fear of putting oneself on the line via a piece of writing, is an illusion, or more precisely a delusion. The piece of writing is seen as a tangible manifestation of one's competence, or lack thereof, a piece of writing that can be evaluated and reevaluated, a piece of writing that endures for endless judgments.
>
> Many people, hardworking and bright people, suffer from this problem. Never putting their pages on the line, never "going public," they can retain the illusion that they are indeed brilliant or, conversely, they can protect themselves from being publicly revealed for the truly mediocre minds they in fact fear themselves to be. Curiously, these two diametrically opposed motivations often operate within the same individual and, moreover, often operate almost simultaneously. It's the old syndrome—"remain silent and you might appear a fool; open your mouth and you remove all doubt."

One reason for the fear that "They won't like what I've written" is the mistaken notion that you and your writing are one. You are not your writing. Your writing is a product. It *may* express your own ideas, but a great deal of nonfiction writing presents facts and other people's ideas. If you are pleased with what you are writing and how it is expressed, you will be more confident about the reactions that others have to your writing. Criticisms will be viewed as criticisms of your writing, not of *you* personally.

Another myth behind "They won't like what I've written" is humorously expressed by Dennis Palumbo in his essay, "A Writer's Guide to Not Writing," published in the July 16, 1978, *Los Angeles Times.* Palumbo points out a truism for many writers, that what you write may not be as terrific as what you had hoped to write:

> Most writers keep notes on things they *intend* to write. Like long-term insurance policies, a file of story ideas gives the writer the illusion of a future. It's what we have instead of a Great Second Half.
>
> But some writers have become so expert at outlining future projects that the actual writing becomes an annoyance. . . .
>
> The solution is simple: Never actually write any of the things you propose. Jot down the ideas, kick them around with your friends, Telex them to distant relatives. Anything but write them. They always sound better when described, anyway. Most things in life do.

By using Myth 6 as a reason for writer's block you create a self-fulfilling prophecy. If your boss expects you to write a report and you fail to do so, your boss may not like you; he may even fire you. Being open to criticism of your writing as you write and rewrite will help you to minimize how devastated you will feel if someone does *not* like your writing. View criticism not as emotion-laden but simply as feedback—a neutral concept.

Until you have the courage to go out on a limb and express your own ideas, depend more on research and the views of others. In the beginning, stick to the facts. If you are timid about criticism, let someone else do the preaching.

MYTH 7: "I'LL WRITE AS SOON AS I GET AROUND TO IT"

The problem with letting this theory, a camouflage for procrastination, inhibit your writing is that you may *never* find time to write. Procrastination means doing one thing—probably something enjoyable—when you should be doing something else—usually unpleasant. If you dislike writing, or feel threatened by it, you will be more likely to procrastinate about doing it. If you have trouble even *knowing* that you are procrastinating about writing, consider setting up a writing schedule, or a series of deadlines that you have to fulfill. Check your schedule every day; if you miss your deadline, make sure you note it on your daily calendar. Do not remove reminders about your writing deadline until you have the finished product, however long it takes.

You might also try the reward system to conquer your procrastination problem. Decide in advance what reward you will give yourself if you start, stay with, and complete a writing task. Write down the task you have to do:

To do: _____

Now decide on what you will reward yourself with after you've done it:

My reward will be: _____

Make sure the reward that you decide on is something you truly enjoy so you will have the motivation to keep at your necessary writing task. You might also consider allowing yourself to procrastinate, but only for a few hours or days. By controlling the procrastination, and making this unconscious tendency a conscious one, you will find it easier to return to the writing task at hand.

MYTH 8: "I CAN'T WRITE UNLESS I CAN DO IT EVERY DAY"

Writing is not a biological need. It is unnecessary to write every day, although the more you write, the easier it becomes. One sometime writer, for example, says that the only time she blocks is after she's put her writing down to go on vacation; it's hard to start up again when she returns. The important thing to remember, however, is that skipping a day, a week, or even a month is not an excuse for failing to write when you have to or want to. There are no hard rules about when to write, or even how long to write. Some writers in my survey answered the question about how many hours they write each day with specific numbers, such as "one to three," "two," "five," or "five to six hours." More typical responses were: "Varies—zero to sixteen" or "Too variable to state a specific figure. Some days it's *all* day, maybe ten to twelve hours, other days it's *no* writing per se." Find your own pace and schedule, or lack of one, but write, rewrite, and revise.

The myth that you should write every day may stem from the start-up problems that some writers describe. Interestingly, the start-up problem may be behind the inability-to-stop syndrome that afflicts some writer-workaholics. George, a character in Thomas Wolfe's novel *You Can't Go Home Again*, eloquently expresses how the start-up problem causes some writers to continue beyond their physical limitations:

> . . . you work [write] because you're afraid not to. You work because you have to drive yourself to such a fury to begin. That part's just plain hell! It's so hard to get started that once you do you're afraid of slipping back. You'd rather do anything than go through all that agony again—so you keep going—you keep going faster all the time—you keep going till you couldn't stop even if you wanted to. You forget to eat, to shave, to put on a clean shirt when you have one. You almost forget to sleep, and when you do try to you can't—because the avalanche has started, and it keeps going night and day. . . .

Since starting up is so difficult, some writers would rather work around the clock, until the project, even a book-length manuscript, is done, sometimes finding they have resultant temporary or prolonged burnout (the inability to work at all). Throughout this book you will learn techniques to help you start up *and* stop your writing. One technique is to work in self-contained units with natural divisons, stopping when you have completed a writing-related activity, like planning or doing an outline, or when a section, a chapter, or a first draft is completed. The tendency to block because you do not write every day, or to put off starting because you've lost your place, is minimized, because you have a clear idea of where to begin next time you resume your writing.

SOLUTIONS FOR WRITER'S BLOCK

> Hire someone to put a gun to your head.
> —Administrator who has had writer's block for four years

Is there a pattern to your blocks, or are you so insecure about writing that right now you cannot (will not) write at all? It might be useful for you to analyze when you block, and why it occurs. Your writer's blocks may simply be a time-management problem: Are you scheduling time for writing, as you would for returning phone calls, attending meetings, jogging, or having dinner? Perhaps you are out of sync with your own rhythms: One student broke through her evening blocks when the newspaper she spent two hours reading each morning went on strike and she instead used that time to write. Experiment a little. You may write best right after lunch, and clam up at night. Are there parts of the writing process that you find easier than others, such as writing the first draft versus revising the last draft, doing original research versus library research? Perhaps you could do the easier parts first, to get yourself going, rather than allowing a prolonged block to take hold. Are your writer's blocks tied to personal problems that you are allowing to interfere with your concentration? One professional writer in my survey wrote that fifteen years of psychoanalysis helped her to eliminate her writer's blocks. That is an extreme, costly, and time-consuming solution. Generally, just recognizing a pattern to your writing blocks, or becoming more relaxed and confident about writing in general, will make it easier for you to avoid blocks (or quickly get over them if and when they do occur).

The rest of this chapter will discuss some tried-and-true techniques for dealing with writer's block. Some may work for you, some may not, and you may invent antiblocking techniques of your own. Knowing about these possible solutions for writer's block, however, is like having a supply of celery and carrots in the refrigerator if you are on a diet and need a snack to avoid a food binge.

Freewrite

Ideally, writing should come as naturally to you as speaking. "I don't have anything to say" or "I'm afraid of what people will say about what I've written" interfere with the free flow of your thoughts and ideas. Freewriting, a technique popularized by college English professor Peter Elbow, among others, tries to restore the free flow of words that every literate person should have. Freewriting emphasizes the act of writing, not the end product.

Bernard Asbell, a professional nonfiction writer who also lectures on writer's block, recommends freewriting as a cure for writer's block. "Start writing about anything," Asbell suggests. "If at the end of five seconds you don't know what to write about, write about not knowing what to write about." In *Writing With Power*, Elbow recommends ten minutes of freewriting. Elbow explains:

> To do a freewriting exercise, simply force yourself to write without stopping for ten minutes. Sometimes you will produce good writing, but that's not the goal. Sometimes you will produce garbage, but that's not the goal either. . . . Freewriting helps you learn to write when you don't feel like writing. It is practice in setting deadlines for yourself, taking charge of yourself, and learning gradually how to get that special energy that sometimes comes when you work fast under pressure.

I conducted a fifteen-minute freewriting session with sixteen college professors and graduate students; at least three had been blocked for more than a year. Everyone was able to write about something on command; most did not want to stop when the time was up, and all were surprised that fifteen minutes had already passed since they had started.

On your own, try to apply freewriting directly to the writing you are blocking about. Give yourself a time limit. Freewrite all your thoughts, knowledge, or feelings about that topic. Continue writing until the time limit. Then go back over your freewrite. This freewrite may become your first draft. If you find it hard to begin with the first sentence or paragraph, write the ending. Or write the middle section. No matter where you begin, get something down on paper.

Reward System

Try the reward system. "If I finish a paragraph of this report today, I will. . . ."

Karate-Chop Method

Try the "karate-chop" system, as psychologist Lynn Diamond calls it. You don't have to deal with writing the entire report, brochure, book, or whatever, you just have to do a part of the writing task, a step at a time. If the size of the writing task is awesome, break it down into smaller, more manageable parts. If you're blocked on doing business or personal correspondence, address the envelopes that you will be using. If you are overwhelmed by the report that you have to write, develop an outline, plan what research you will do, and decide what interviews you will conduct. A student who consulted me about being blocked on her term paper took my advice that she begin breaking through her block by typing up the paper's bibliography.

Set Deadlines

Based upon my research into writer's block, blocking seems to be tied to lacking, or having unrealistic, deadlines. Lack of a deadline often leads to indefinite procrastination. An unrealistically short deadline seems to lead to panic and unproductive anxiety. If your employer or teacher has not given you a specific deadline—"Get it in when you can" or "It's due sometime before the end of the semester"—create your own deadline. This final deadline, however, should have interim deadlines—e.g., "I will have the outline completed by *x* date," "I will have the first draft completed by *x* date."

Professor Elbow suggests dividing the time allotted for a writing project in half, allowing half the time for writing and the other half for rewriting. Except for the simplest letter or memo, however, most nonfiction projects will also require you to allot time for conducting research and incorporating critical reviews of your work into your drafts.

Befriend Your Inner Critics

Setting high standards for your writing—and wishing to meet those standards—can be an excellent way to become a better writer. If your inner critics are too harsh, however, you may have frequent writer's blocks. You need to learn how to harness your inner critics so they facilitate, not inhibit, your writing.

View Writing as a Process

Allow yourself to come alive during the writing process. Writer's block can result from rigidly holding on to a preconceived idea of what should be said and how it should be written.

Distinguish Between Resting and Blocking

Recognize the difference between when a break from writing is necessary and when you are actually blocking. Isobel Silden, a successful magazine writer and columnist, explains how she recognizes and deals with these two situations:

> On the rare occasions when I'd rather scuffle through leaves, or read a good book, I suppose one could construe that as writer's block, so I give in to it: I read the good book, or I scuff. I think it's my body's way of telling me my brain needs a rest. And after a couple of hours I'm ready to sit back here at my typewriter. If it goes on too long, and it sometimes has happened that I wanted to goof off for a day or two while deadlines were looming, this is my trick: I go into meditation and come to center, to ascertain what is bothering me, or to work out whatever blocks are at work in my subconscious. After a few minutes' meditation, I am mentally refreshed. Whatever challenges there may have been have resolved themselves, and again my typewriter and I are inseparable. From my brain through my fingers onto the nice white pages.

Use a Tape Recorder

Talking into a tape recorder might help you to break through your writer's block. Free-associate on the topic you are blocked about. Don't concern yourself with punctuation or using the perfect word. Transcribe the tape. It might become a first draft. At least you will have something on paper. I used this method to break through a very serious block that I was having when finishing my book *Victims*, about victims of major violent and property crimes. The preface to the book was to recapitulate the effect of the murder of my brother on my family. Day after day my attempts to get something down on paper were futile; I sat and stared at the typewriter or began to cry. The rest of the book was finished and my editor needed the preface to put the book into production. I was determined to write that preface, and so at four o'clock one morning I turned on the tape recorder and spoke into it all my thoughts, feelings, and recollections. Of course when I transcribed the tape the material was out of order and in need of several revisions, but at least it was there to be molded and shaped.

Clarify Your Reasons for Writing

When all else fails, remember the punishments that may occur if you give in to a writer's block: disappointed employers, a reputation for being fast on promises and short on delivery. As one blocked sometime writer says: "The pain of noncompletion is often greater than the pain of putting pen to paper."

Become More Confident

Increase your confidence in yourself as a writer and you will probably decrease your tendency to block. The next chapters will help you to bolster your writing-related confidence level. Do not, however, minimize the benefits of having an outside editor on tap. Knowing you can show your writing to someone whose editing and critical abilities you value may help you to feel less inhibited about writing. This person can be a friend, a paid freelance editor, or someone in your company whose job it is to edit or critique writing. If you know that your first draft (or third or fourth) will be read carefully by eyes other than your own, it may help you to free up and freewrite.

Complaining about writer's block ensures its prolongation. Avoid talking about it. Put that energy into writing instead. Write about the block, if necessary. The only cure for having something to write coupled with an inability or unwillingness to write it is, alas, to succeed in writing it.

EXERCISES

1. Freewrite about anything for twenty minutes. Don't stop to edit or rewrite. Now go back and reread your freewrite. Is it interesting? Well written? Organized? Note two or three ways you could improve this freewrite. Date the freewrite and save it for later review.

2. For ten minutes, freewrite about anything or anyone you are knowledgeable about, such as your job, a hobby, a favorite vacation spot. Put it aside for a few days. Later, when you reread it, ask yourself if there are ways you could make it more informative, persuasive, or entertaining. Date this freewrite and save it for rewriting after you have read the chapter on research.

3. If you have a tendency to procrastinate about your writing, pick one of the above projects, or another one that you have been meaning to do, and write down the title of the project in the space below. Then list the consequences to you—personal, professional, emotional, or financial—for delaying this writing.

   Writing project:_____
   Consequences of procrastinating:
   _____
   _____
   _____

   Set a deadline for completing this writing task, and decide on a reward that you will give yourself for doing it.

4. In your nonfiction journal, freewrite a paragraph about how your ideas about nonfiction writing have changed by reading (and doing the practice exercises) thus far in *How to Write Like a Professional.*

5. Consider creating a schedule for your writing, mapping

out one or more hours that you will devote consistently to writing. Like any skill, your writing will benefit from regular practice and a fixed routine.

REFERENCES

Ellis, Albert, and William J. Knaus. *Overcoming Procrastination.* New York: New American Library, 1977. An outgrowth of Ellis's rational-emotional therapy (RET) approach, the authors' insights and suggestions could easily be applied to any writing task.

Mack, Karin, and Eric Skjei. *Overcoming Writing Blocks.* Los Angeles: J.P. Tarcher, Inc., 1979. The authors suggest that writer's block occurs because: (1) Writing is hard work; (2) Writing invites judgment by others; and (3) Writing "evokes your own powerful chorus of internal critics." Some of their suggestions for unblocking—preparing to write, organizing, writing the rough draft, revising and polishing—are solid guidelines for creating any piece of writing. Others—systematic relaxation strategies, getting to know the internal critic—are useful ways to approach this problem.

Safán-Gerard, Desy. "How to Unblock." *Psychology Today* (January 1978), pp. 78, 81, 83, 85–6. A discussion of the group therapy sessions that Safán-Gerard conducts with artists who are blocked, with useful insights for writers as well.

3

Tools of the Trade

Like a cabinetmaker who wants to carve a chest, a writer needs certain tools to build words, sentences, and paragraphs. As with any craft, it is advisable to use tools that make you feel comfortable, and that help you do the best job. If a pad and pencil work for you, fine. If the thought of retyping your writing inhibits you from doing multiple rewrites, consider using a word processor, becoming a faster typist, or hiring a typist.

The tools you use to write may be a reflection of your typing skills, your personality, or your income level. I recall that in my early twenties, deciding what typestyle to select for my new $250 electric typewriter loomed as large in my mind as which $3,000 word processor to select seems to for today's writers. What tools you need also depends on whether the methods you have been using serve you well enough. Connecticut-based Claire Safran, an established freelance magazine writer and a roving editor for *Reader's Digest,* discusses her own simple approach to writer's tools and references:

> I really don't have many tools. I have a standard electric type-writer, a telephone, and paper. That's about it. I don't have a lot of reference books, but I do have a library card that I use often. I also have access to a psychiatric library at a nearby hospital, helpful for me, where I can see all the current professional journals. [The only time] I used an outside typist [was] when I had a broken hand and couldn't manage on my own. Other than that, I tend to type up my final draft myself. I find that as I'm doing the final draft to send to the editor, I see things I might have missed up to that point, so it's a helpful pressure for doing a kind of final polish.
>
> I think writers today are too obsessed with tools. It seems the only thing that writers want to talk about when they get together now is the word processor and how it's making them more effi-

cient. I worry about writers who want to be too efficient. I don't think writing is an efficient task. I don't know that the computer makes anyone a better writer. Until Isaac Bashevis Singer gives up his pen and paper for the computer, I won't be convinced.

CRAYONS TO WORD PROCESSORS

When deciding on what tools to use when you write, keep in mind the following considerations:

- The audience for your writing (personal, business, or school)
- Personal preferences (pen, pencil, typewriter, word processor)
- Available support services (Will you do everything yourself, or do you have access to a typist or secretary?).
- Finances

The Audience

Although computers are now generating "form" love letters, in most cases you should probably still stick to pen and paper for such intimate writing. There are, of course, exceptions: A corporate executive I interviewed would like to send handwritten notes but his penmanship is so poor that he has to print, or, reluctantly, send typed personal notes or letters. By contrast, most business or school writing tasks require you to type your manuscript.

Personal Taste

Some prefer to dictate a first draft, type it or have it typed, and edit and rewrite from the transcript. Others need to write and edit in longhand and then have the draft typed, or type it themselves. Some compose directly at the typewriter or keyboard and edit each draft. In the last few years, at work and at home, word processors have begun to replace typewriters as the tool of choice for writing. Editing can be done on the screen or on each hardcopy version that the printer spits out.

Support Services

An executive with a secretary can write in longhand, or dictate and have a tape transcribed and typed, more easily than someone who works alone. You will find it convenient to have a photocopying machine nearby. If you work at home, you might find the trips to the photocopy store a welcome break from your writing.

Finances

Although a word processor may have long-term advantages in terms of speed and efficiency, the initial financial outlay is far greater than for pencil and paper or even a typewriter. Prices have come down fast, however. A system that would have cost $6,000 two years ago is now available for less than $3,000; new systems are being introduced for less than $1,000. However, a manual typewriter can be purchased for under $100, and an electric typewriter for less than $200. To spread out costs, some writers actually band together to purchase a computer jointly and share time on it.

Although a word processor cannot write for you, it can make the revising part of writing easier; in that way it may encourage additional rewriting, which may in turn improve your writing. You may be perfectly content with your manual or electric typewriter; you may long for a memory typewriter or a word processor, or you may already have access to one. Remember that a word processor may save you time in the long run, but in the short run, you will need to devote some time to learning how to use your system. A freelance writer who has had her $2,000 word processor for several months explains why it is sitting untouched in the corner of her office:

> I still don't know how to use it. I now realize that the most important thing for someone buying a word processor is to be sure you can get the machine serviced right away if there's a problem with it. The second thing is to be sure there is someone to answer your questions about how to use it. I'm not yet computer literate. . . . Once I learn how to use the computer, however, I know I'll be glad I have it. I look forward to the change. The major

drawback of a typewriter is the constant [re]typing when you're trying to get something done. In the long run, the computer will be economically viable.

Mechanical helpers can be time-saving tools, but they can also be trouble, especially in the beginning. If you want to switch over from a typewriter to a computer/word processor, build into your work schedule the learning time that you will need to gain mastery over it, including careful study of the user's manual. Initially, it may take more—not less—time to write something, but eventually writing, especially rewriting, will be faster and easier for you. I spent several weeks learning how to use my word processor and, truthfully, at least six more months until I was saving rather than spending time because of it. Now, almost three years later, I find it almost inconceivable that I ever used a typewriter. Not only has my productivity improved, but my entire way of conducting research, writing, and rewriting has been affected positively. I don't have as many backaches as in the days when I typed and retyped for hours on end. With computerized retrieval systems, I have pruned down my files, eliminating the little pieces of paper I always intended to put "somewhere," even eliminating the necessity of a Rolodex. On two thin floppy disks I have thousands of names and addresses.

If you do get a word processor, remember these three cautionary notes:

1. Save your text periodically, so you won't "lose" it if there's a power failure.
2. Make backup copies of your writing; if a disk is defective, you won't lose your work.
3. The printers that accompany word processors are fast and they can generate hard copy—miles of paper. At first it requires discipline to edit on the screen, printing out only as needed. Also, beware of using printing out as an excuse to waste time: it's easy to think you are writing as clean copy comes out of the printer, when in fact you are merely relaxing.

R.V. Denenberg, a former editor for the *New York Times* and a freelance author, explains that he uses more paper now that he has a computer for writing, but he saves time and writes better:

> I thought it would save paper, but it actually generates more paper. The word processor has resulted in any piece of copy going through many more drafts than before, which improves it. I'm constantly refining from one draft to another. In the past there was simply a physical barrier to how many times I could get a clean copy of my editing. My printer is able to turn out a copy of a whole book manuscript in an hour and a half. At that rate, I can easily afford to say every few days, "Okay, let's have a fresh copy of it. Let's see where we stand now." In the past it wasn't possible to retype the whole book several times. Also, if I gave the manuscript out to a typist, it had to be away for a week. Now, I can go out and have a cup of coffee, come back, and have a copy of the book.
>
> The only disadvantages of a word processor are in the beginning, when you have accidents that cause you to lose copy. You have disks that go bad on you and you haven't backed them up. Or you have power failures and you lose a few pages on the screen. However, after everything bad has happened to you, you learn how to protect yourself.

In his best-selling book *The Word Processing Book: A Short Course in Computer Literacy* (Los Angeles: Prelude Press, 1982), Peter A. McWilliams lists these ten advantages of word processors for writers. (My comments—in brackets—are provided for clarity.)

1. Change is effortless.
2. Retyping is unnecessary.
3. Spelling is perfect. [Programs that check spelling are available.]
4. Word processors are quiet.
5. You are not chained to a typewriter table. [There are detachable keyboards so you can work lying down, or even outside or in another room.]
6. No more carriage returns.
7. Correspondence is easy. [By changing only the name, you can use the same body of a letter without retyping.]
8. Research is easier. [Data banks minimize trips to the library.]

9. Other programs are available. [A writer is exposed to a great variety of materials, including music programs, video games, adventure stories, etc.]
10. They're fun.

McWilliams says a word processor has made writing "a joy" for him, rather than the "chore" it used to be. I am personally convinced that word processors will become as common equipment for writers as typewriters are today. Software for managing research, doing statistics, and checking spelling enables you to accomplish more in less time. A computer that recognizes your voice, and types out your words, will eventually be available for writers who want to avoid typing even the first draft. Computers and word processors certainly bring writing, long considered a creative act outside the realm of gadgets and technological jargon, into the electronic age. However, although it facilitates writing, especially rewriting, the word processor does not automatically make you a better writer.

If you are thinking about acquiring a system, consider taking a course in word processing or computer use, but try to take a course about the particular system you are thinking of investing in. There are, of course, general concepts that apply to all systems, such as saving and moving your text, but each system has specific details that must be mastered. You might also consider joining a users group in your local community, such as "Apple Users Groups" for owners of Apple computers. You might also subscribe to magazines for owners of your system, such as *Nibble* for Apple owners, or general computer magazines, such as *Popular Computing*.

Here is a checklist of the range of tools that a nonfiction writer might consider owning, or having available:

Paper
    Pads (and stationery) for handwritten materials
    Twenty-pound weight typing paper
    Letterhead
Envelopes
    To match letterhead
    Oversized (9 × 12, 10 × 13 inches) for mailing out manuscripts

For returns when soliciting responses
Pencils
Pen
Typewriter (manual or electric) or word processor and printer
Tape recorder or dictation machine (the smaller the better)
    Tapes
    Batteries, battery pack, cord for use off house current
Filing system for research
    (5 × 8-inch index cards, file folders, computerized)
Recording system for research, assignments, notes
Optional
    35mm camera and flash
    Camera with instant development capabilities
Daily writing journal

THE NONFICTION WRITER'S LIBRARY

You may want to surround yourself with thousands of reference books, or you may prefer to go to the library as needed. That is a choice dependent on personal taste, finances, and available bookshelf space. There are a few books that any nonfiction writer should have at his or her fingertips for instant fact, spelling, or style checks:

- Dictionary
- Thesaurus
- Book of familiar quotations
- World atlas
- World almanac
- One-volume general encyclopedia
- Grammar reference

Consider, too, some books about style: Strunk and White's *The Elements of Style* and Sheridan Baker's *The Complete Stylist*, for example. Depending on your needs, research guides like Barzun and Graff's *The Modern Researcher* (New York: Harcourt Brace Jovanovich, Inc., 1977), and journals, magazines, and books in your area of expertise may also be useful. Writing nonfiction involves handling a lot of facts, staying organized as you accumulate those facts, and managing your time. You might, therefore, want to look at articles and books in those areas, such as Stephanie Winston's *Getting Organized* and Alan Lakein's *How To Get Control of Your Time and Your Life.*

As you accumulate more and more research for your writing, you will need to create an organized system for retrieving information as needed in the writing stages of your work. The faster you can find the facts, quotes, or references that you need, the more efficient you will be as a writer. I personally like to have as many directories, reference books, journals, textbooks, and popular and scholarly books at my fingertips as I can physically store in my home. Even the best office or home library, however, should not substitute for outside libraries, especially specialized ones; it is impossible for any individual to compete with the up-to-date variety of the resources of those institutions.

A PLACE FOR WRITING

The trick for making your work environment conducive to writing, whether it is at home or in an office, is to be organized. The top of your desk should be free from clutter, whether that "desk" is a dining room table or a Queen Anne desk. Your typewriter or word processor should be on a separate desk or table; the first desk is where you think, plan, and spread out. If possible, it should be large.

Organizing the top of your desk sans typewriter/word processor is quite an individual affair. If you have a problem concentrating at your desk, try experimenting with adding or removing items to see if your work habits improve. Juggle family photographs, stapler, pencil holder, electric pencil sharpener, paper weights, and calendars, for example. You should avoid keeping anything other than your current writing project on top of your desk—too many files or projects can provoke a "doing too much at once" syndrome. Thomas Wolfe supposedly wrote his novels on top of his refrigerator, and others get rid of their second desks and use counter tops, or sit on the sofa, instead. However, if you're typical in this respect, you'll want at least one basic desk. I once interviewed a former advertising executive who had become a successful freelance writer; he had written more than twenty books in the previous five years. We spoke in his basement office beside his two desks. Each desk had its own typewriter and was devoted to a different project. If he got bored or blocked on one, he turned to the other. He also saved the start-up time that would have been necessary if he had had to switch projects at one desk.

If you write at home, and you live with others, it will be imperative for you to become and remain organized, since family members may have access to your office. Some writers have a very strong prohibition against *any* visitors to their writing area, a philosophy reflected by nonfiction writer and teacher Hayes B. Jacobs in *Writing and Selling Non-Fiction* (Cincinnati: Writer's Digest Books, 1968):

> Find some place in your house or apartment, put all your writing equipment, reference books, notes, etc., in it, and regard it as a priest would his altar. It is your private, holy place. Be priestly, and devoted. Keep out all intruders. Erect "Off Limits" signs—literally, if necessary. Keep out children, mates, friends, cleaning women. At the appointed hour [that you have designated for writing], *be* there in your "place," then get to work. Speak to no one and allow no one to speak to you. Adjust your appetite, and yes, your bathroom habits (the astronauts do, and so can you) so that you have no possible excuse to leave your "place" until the time is up. I promise that you will be surprised at what you will be able to accomplish.

If a separate room for writing is impractical, you might consider purchasing a complete office in a cabinet, sold by many furniture companies to solve the space and organizational problems of those who must work in multifunctional areas. These cabinets open to display specific areas for such writing needs as filing cabinets, reference materials, supplies, a typewriter, even an office phone. When closed, the unit resembles a big box. This approach may not do wonders for your decor, but it might solve the problem of having all your writing tools and reference materials in one place.

Organizing your writing environment will be quite a different endeavor depending on whether your home office is a separate room in a large home or the corner of the bedroom in a one-bedroom apartment that houses a family of three. Some considerations are universal, however: What are the essential supplies and pieces of equipment that have to be nearby, and what can be stored elsewhere—in closets, bookcases, other rooms, even other locations?

There are physical and social problems inherent in a writer's work environment that you should consider. Alternating working at home, at your office, or even at the library may be a solution that results in a more pleasant life-style, with long-term emotional and social benefits, even if it seems less productive than total isolation and seclusion. Newspaper reporter Drew Fetherston describes how much more difficult he found writing when, for nine years, he was out of the newsroom and more removed from other writers:

> I worked in isolation in Investigations, which is an office down the hall removed from the City Room. One or two reporters there or none a lot of the time. . . . I found myself resenting the fact that to get a little bit of human company I had to get up, leave my work, and walk down the hall and find somebody to socialize with a little bit. . . . I think it's more refreshing to write a little bit, take a break, write a little bit more, and take a break. Having other people around just creates situations where you can take that break when it presents itself.

Gail Schiller Tuchman, formerly an editor at Macmillan Publishing Company and now a freelance children's book writer, notes how, within limits, you can discipline yourself to write anywhere, and anytime, if you have to:

> My two-year-old daughter's up from six or seven in the morning till eight or nine at night and wants a lot of attention, so it's very difficult to work with her around. The only way that I can make the time and space [to write] is to have a babysitter come in for a couple of hours a day, or to work late in the evening. Whether or not that's my creative time—my creative time may be in the morning but I may have the sitter available from three to six—I have to force myself to be creative during the three-to-six period, get my inspiration, and discipline myself to write during the time that I have some free space. [Despite these limitations], in one year I've written over a dozen children's picture books with a

collaborator, I have been working on an art book, and I've been doing freelance writing for publishers. It's been great.

Decide on the tools, reference books, and work environments that will facilitate your writing. (If you write in two places—in your office and at home—you may need multiple copies of certain references, such as the dictionary or atlas, as well as two operational writing environments.) If you do a lot of traveling, you might want to have a writer's traveling kit ready to go:

1. Portable typewriter or word processor
2. Paper
3. Tape recorder for dictating
4. A compact dictionary and thesaurus
5. Supplies, such as scissors, paper clips, tape, liquid eraser or correction paper.

At home, or on the road, feeling confident about your tools of the trade will aid the writing process; that, in turn, will improve your final products.

EXERCISES

1. Take stock of your home or office library and borrow or buy the books you need to accommodate your nonfiction writing needs.

2. Do you have a current library card? Are you familiar with the special libraries, nearby or in other cities, that you might want to consult for a current or future writing project? If you are a college graduate, and live near your school, find out if you can pay a small charge for annual library privileges at your alma mater.

3. Make a written plan, or draw a sketch, for an ideal work environment in which you will do your writing. Consider the criteria listed at the beginning of this chapter and create, or rearrange, the environments in which you now work according to those factors.

REFERENCES

Baker, Sheridan. *The Complete Stylist.* New York: Crowell, 1966.

Barkas, J.L. *Creative Time Management.* Englewood Cliffs: Prentice-Hall, Inc., 1984.

Bartlett, John. *Bartlett's Familiar Quotations,* 14th ed. Edited by Emily Morison Beck. Boston: Little, Brown, and Company, 1968. Hundreds of quotations arranged chronologically by the year of the work or the author, such as the Bible, Shakespeare, and Whitman. Indexed.

Cassill, Kay. *The Complete Handbook for Freelance Writers.* Cincinnati: Writer's Digest Books, 1981. See especially Chapter 4, "Space, Tools, and Equipment."

Lakein, Alan. *How to Get Control of Your Time and Your Life.* New York: New American Library, 1973.

Lewis, Norman, ed. *The New Roget's Thesaurus in Dictionary Form.* New York: Berkley Publishing Corporation, 1977. This thesaurus is based on C.O. Sylvester Mawson's alphabetical arrangement of the famous Roget system of word classification.

McWhiter, Norris, ed. *Guinness Book of World Records.* New York: Sterling Publishing Company, Inc. (updated annually).

McWilliams, Peter A. *The Word Processing Book.* Los Angeles: Prelude Press, 1982.

Mitchell, James, and Jess Stein, eds. *The Random House Encyclopedia,* Rev. ed. New York: Random House, Inc., 1983. A one-volume, illustrated three-thousand-page reference book.

Oxford Dictionary of Quotations, 2nd ed. New York: Oxford University Press, 1953.

Partnow, Elaine, ed. *The Quotable Woman (1800–1975).* Los Angeles: Corwin Books, 1977. Quotes from such notable women as Marie Curie, Harriet Tubman, and Sylvia Townsend Warner.

Webster's New Dictonary of Synonyms. Springfield, Mass.: G.&C. Merriam Company, 1973.

Webster's Third New International Dictionary, Unabridged. Springfield, MA: G.&C. Merriam Company, 1981.

Winston, Stephanie, *Getting Organized.* New York: Warner Books, 1979.

World Almanac and Book of Facts, The. New York: Newspaper Enterprise Association, Inc. (updated annually). A leading one-volume information guide, published since 1868.

4

Content

There are two things wrong with almost all legal writing. One
is its style. The other is its content.
—Professor Fred Rodell, "Goodbye to Law Reviews,"
Virginia Law Review

You have to have something to say when you speak; the
same holds true for when you write. *What* you write is the content in expository writing; *how* you write it is the style. Of course
there is considerable overlap in these two arbitrary categories:
Punctuation and grammatical considerations are both content
and style issues. Furthermore, an idea or topic will affect the style
of your writing, just as particular types of writing (such as memos,
reports, letters, or books) and certain audiences (such as an employer or your beloved) or markets (like the *Journal of the American Medical Association* or *Redbook*) affect your content.

In this chapter, the focus will be on generating and improving ideas for your writing, and on conducting research. Following
a discussion of thought content, this chapter will provide an understanding of basic primary and secondary research skills to help
you with the *what* part of expository writing. Research embraces
the extremes of sitting in a musty library taking notes from secondary sources, to going into the jungles of Brazil to collect original data. Somewhere in between, however, is research that is
practical and do-able, yet exciting, eye-opening, and adventurous.
Whether your audience is a boss, friend, teacher, editor, or the
anonymous public, the content of your nonfiction writing can be
memorable.

IDEAS

If the content of your writing is solid, however rough your style, your writing will be superior to eloquent sentences embodying faulty or vacuous thoughts. John S. Fielden emphasizes this point in "What Do You Mean I Can't Write?," a classic article that appeared in the May-June 1964 *Harvard Business Review*:

> ... There is no substitute for the thought content of a communication. What good is accomplished if a message is excellent in all the other respects we have discussed—if it is readable, correct, and appropriate—yet the content is faulty? It can even do harm, if the other aspects succeed in disguising the fact that it is superficial, stupid, or biased. The superior receiving it may send it up through the organization with his signature, or, equally serious, he may make an important (and disastrous) decision based on it.
> ... The discipline of translating thoughts into words and organizing these thoughts logically has no equal as intellectual training. For there is one slogan that is true: "Disorganized, illogical writing reflects a disorganized, illogical (and untrained) mind."

Your first concern in writing nonfiction is, therefore, "What shall I write about?" or "What do I want to say?" At work or in school, your employer or teacher may provide you with the writing idea or assignment. "Write a memo about the conference you want us to sponsor," your boss says. "It's a good policy to follow up meetings with new clients with a goodwill letter," your supervisor suggests. "Your report is due by the end of January," your teacher commands. These kinds of writing ideas can be deemed *reactive* ones, since they depend on work, school, or personal responsibilities. Although reactive writing tasks are usually assigned to you, you will still benefit from suggestions for sharpening those ideas and strengthening them with research or stylistic flourishes, as will be discussed in this and the next two chapters.

There are other ideas—ones you generate yourself—that can be labled *active* ones. These ideas may relate to specific work, school, or personal matters, or may be self-starting projects, such as contacting a long-lost high school friend or getting your ideas published in the company newsletter, or in a journal, a magazine, or a book.

There are ideas all around you for active writing projects. The advice that most writing teachers give—"Write about what you know best"—is a place to start. What you know, however, is far more than your autobiography; it includes career-related knowledge (whether you are a secretary, physician, management executive, or dog trainer), your parenting expertise, or your hobbies. You might also begin with what you wish to know, such as how to improve communication with your friends or what your family tree reveals. Another suggestion I have about finding ideas is one that has always worked for me, namely, "Write about what you care about." If you follow this guideline, you'll have a better chance of sticking with your idea when the rewriting, or research, gets tough—when the honeymoon phase of conceiving the idea, or completing the first draft, is over and you are involved in the time-consuming ups and downs of fourth or fifth drafts. If you genuinely care about your idea, pursuing your thoughts and stating them as clearly as possible will be that much easier and more satisfying.

Be aware that specific kinds of writing will have definite idea considerations. "Is it topical or timely?" is a question to test an idea against, whether you are thinking of a nonfiction book, a congratulations, condolence, or thank-you letter, or a grant proposal. Of course, there will be numerous writing ideas that you might consider but have to reject because of ethical, political, or financial limitations.

Writing ideas, however, are not good or bad per se; how you develop an idea will make the difference. Something as potentially trite as "the conflict between motherhood and a career," given a fresh approach, may be as intriguing as an essay on a futuristic trend only you know about. As you will see in concrete detail in Chapter 6, your execution of even the most mundane reactive idea, like a monthly report, improves if you ask yourself basic questions, such as: "Is this interesting?" "Is this fresh and new?" "Are my arguments well conceived and substantiated?" "Why should someone bother to read this?" and "Who is my audience?"

I have discovered that the most common idea-related writing problem is picking too broad a topic, such as "racism," "unemployment," "dating," or "computers." Unless you have several years to devote to your idea, or a team of assistants, too general an idea almost guarantees a superficial and unimpressive piece of writing. Instead, pick a concrete and specific subject, not a vague one, or rethink your reactive topic, such as a letter soliciting new business, highlighting one or two selling statements or concepts. Lean toward narrow, not broad, writing themes. Find a specific issue within a general one; you will be less likely to write generalizations and clichés. If you want to write something about improving corporate efficiency, for example, consider writing about the four-day week, or electronic mail. You will probably get more attention than if you write a general indictment of poor productivity at the office.

If you are completely blocked about ideas to write about, try to get your thoughts flowing by commenting in your daily non-fiction journal on a specific newspaper story, media report, or a book or cultural event that has something to do with your own professional or personal concerns. You might also get ideas to stimulate writing projects from the press releases describing new products or research that are sent by public relations firms, university public information offices, and companies. These releases often give the names of researchers or executives to contact for further written information or personal interviews. A short letter to such firms or schools, explaining who you are and why you want to be on their mailing list, may result in a steady stream of sources for potential writing topics. Another way of generating writing ideas may be to interview local residents who make it big, with an eye toward publishing these interviews or features in local newspapers or magazines. Finally, consider initiating personal or company letters, rather than only responding to those in your "in" box. I keep a file labeled "Ideas" in which I keep thoughts I have jotted down that might become newspaper stories, magazine articles, or books. If it seems helpful, I include in that file a copy of the published article or even letter that originally inspired a particular idea. I also keep notes on possible ideas in my daily journals, or, if an idea occurs to me while I'm traveling, in the pad that I keep in my purse. My point is that you should *write down* any writing ideas or assignments, since this gets you writing and stirs your memory if you cannot execute an idea for some time to come.

Here is a sampling of the hundreds of ideas in my "Ideas" file, some of which have been worked into short or long works that I have published:

- A historical overview of the treatment of crime victims in America
- Compulsive talking: what it is and any cures
- Your restaurant rights
- Measuring the impact of verbal abuse
- Multiple-job holders and moonlighting
- How to know if psychotherapy is working, or is even necessary
- An inside look at the advice columnists
- Unnecessary hospital tests
- Should you and your spouse maintain separate residences?
- Love on the rebound: Can it work?
- The writer's catalogue
- From riches to rags: reverse Horatio Alger stories
- New hope for compulsive eaters

In summary, every writing task must consider your idea—*what* you want to say (thoughts); your motive—*why* you want to express this idea (inform, persuade, entertain); and your audience—for *whom* you are writing. These three considerations will of course affect the content of your writing, as well as your style.

Good writing begins with an idea, whatever its source. Thinking through that idea is a challenging but rewarding process. "What is the hardest task in the world?," essayist Ralph Waldo Emerson asks in "Intellect." "To think," he replies. Emerson continues, exploring how writers are able to synthesize what others only experience:

> We are all wise. The difference between persons is not in wisdom but in art. I knew, in an academical club, a person who always deferred to me, who, seeing my whim for writing, fancied that my experiences had somewhat superior; whilst I saw that his experiences were as good as mine. Give them to me and I would make the same use of them. He held the old; he holds the new; I had the habit of tacking together the old and the new which he did not use to exercise. This may hold in the great examples. Perhaps, if we should meet Shakespeare we should not be conscious of any steep inferiority; no, but of a great equality,—only that he possessed a strange skill of using, of classifying his facts, which we lacked. . . .

Carefully consider the thoughts you wish to convey in whatever you are writing—letter, memo, speech, or book. If your thoughts are hazy, your writing will reflect this, at least at first. If your thoughts are distinct, you will still need to write and rewrite until others grasp your meaning—but at least it will be possible for them to do so. If you are and remain unsure of what you want to say, making a clear impression in your reader's mind is impossible. "Writing is embodied thought," scholar Jacques Barzun writes in *On Writing, Editing, and Publishing*, "and the thought is clear or muddy, graspable or fugitive, according to the purity of the medium."

GATHERING INFORMATION (CONDUCTING RESEARCH)

The content of your writing is based on what you already know, or what you find out. You can write off the top of your head—freewrite—or you can collect information and do research. You may already know enough to complete whatever writing task is before you. If that is the case, your content concerns will focus on organizing your material: what to include or leave out, and the order in which to present your facts or opinions. You might also need to check or obtain additional facts. The need for research may be more obvious for certain kinds of nonfiction writing, such as a biography, than for others, such as a first-person essay, but most nonfiction writing relies on primary or secondary research.

We have established that there are two ways of gathering information—obtaining it yourself or relying on the information gathered by others. Research that is firsthand, whether done by you or others, is "primary." Primary research includes interviews and firsthand observations as well as diaries, autobiographies, tapes, and letters written by others that you hear or read. Research that you conduct yourself may be time consuming and costly and is, of course, open to your biases, prejudices, and the limitations of your knowledge. That is the strength of research you conduct yourself, as well as its weakness. Novelist Joan Didion's nonfiction account of the strife in El Salvador was acclaimed because it was based on her interpretation of what she had observed and heard during her stay there. At the opposite extreme would be writing a study of El Salvador based only on secondary sources—such as newspaper reports or government press releases—in which other writers had done all the interpreting for you. A middle-of-the road approach might be to augment secondary sources with long-distance telephone interviews with Salvadorans conducted from your home, in-person interviews done closer to home with those who have emigrated here from there, and first-person accounts that are written or on tape. It is important to realize, however, that research you do yourself is not *inherently* better than material that is already available.

The content of your writing will be based on what you have learned from speaking and hearing; from sight, smell, taste, feeling; and from thinking. Each of these seven skills is tied to research techniques for collecting information:

- Hearing, seeing, speaking: interviews
- Seeing and hearing: observations
- Thinking: reading, use of existing sources, analysis

Determine the content of your writing by answering this question: "Why should someone want to read what I have written?"

You can enhance your thought through style, for example by enlarging it with a metaphor or a simile, or you can improve it with a detail or a quotation you've found in your research. "Research" for a nonfiction writing task may be as simple as checking the spelling of proper names for a business letter, or as complex as making a trip around the world to gather information for a new travel guide. One of the best ways to improve the content of your writing is with quotations from sources that either support or refute your ideas or statements. You can find secondary sources for such material; you can extract quotations from others' primary research; or you can conduct your own in-person or telephone interviews.

Although nonfiction research may cover an enormous range, limitations are imposed by a writer's available time, skills, finances, and support services. To decide whether what you will write about will be based on primary or on secondary research (or some combination of the two), you should consider both the requirements of the topic and practical considerations of the kind mentioned above.

INTERVIEWS

"The exchange of information is the *central* purpose of the interview," writes Raymond L. Gorden in *Interviewing: Strategy, Techniques and Tactics* (Homewood, Illinois: Dorsey Press, 1980). Gorden is emphasizing the difference between an interview and an ordinary conversation. Moreover, the information exchange in an interview is unequal; you are finding out far more than you are revealing—or you should be.

There are three basic kinds of interviews:

1. *For attribution:* You will ascribe quotations or information to the person you are interviewing.
2. *Anonymous:* You will use quotations or information exactly as you are given it, but the name of the person interviewed will not appear, or will be changed.
3. *Background:* You will build your knowledge in an area without using specific quotations or details from the interview.

Obviously, whether or not an interview is for attribution may affect the kind of the information you obtain as well as the motives someone has for agreeing to be interviewed. For example, if you decide to interview a company president, and you plan to use her name in your report, what she says, as well as what information you can ascribe to her, is likely to be "official" information. Because you will be citing her by name, her motives in being interviewed may include a wish to gain favorable publicity for herself and for her company, as well as the flattery and cathartic values of being interviewed. What she says also may be somewhat determined by the use you will have for the interview. If, by contrast, you are doing research on company presidents and you make it clear that you will not use any real names in your written reports, the opinions she expresses, and the information she provides you with, may be quite different. (Even the language she uses may be less carefully chosen.) If the interviewee trusts you, she may tell you things "off the record." Even if her real name is to be used, she is providing you with information that she wants you to have but does not want ascribed to her.

The first question most people ask about interviews is: "How do I get someone to agree to an interview?" Once you have established what you want to learn about—your topic—you next decide to whom you want to talk—a specific individual, an expert, or someone who simply reflects opinion about what you are writing. Next, gaining the cooperation of a complete stranger, famous or not, will be a challenging task. Your writing skills, if you write a letter asking for the interview, will be called into play. You will want to briefly explain what you are doing, why you want the interview, what use you will make of it, and, as persuasively as possible, one or more reasons your potential subject (interviewee) should grant you the interview.

In summary, when you approach a possible interviewee, whether through a letter, in person, or over the phone, you should briefly include the following information in your first few moments of interaction:

1. Who you are
2. For whom you are conducting the interview (your company, your school, yourself)
3. The purpose of the interview
4. Why you are asking that specific person and how you went about selecting him or her
5. Whether or not the interview will be for attribution or anonymous and confidential

Over the years, I have conducted hundreds of interviews with celebrities (Cliff Robertson, Dina Merrill, Willem de Kooning, Harold Pinter, Jerome Hines and others) and with experts (criminologist Marvin E. Wolfgang and psychiatrists Avodah Offit and the late Fredric Wertham), as well as with persons whose anonymity was assured. The letter that follows led to dozens of anonymous and confidential in-person and telephone interviews for my Ph.D. dissertation:

Dear ———,

I am conducting interviews for my Ph.D. dissertation. A copy of the letter from the Executive Officer of my department is attached. I am interviewing women on the Upper East Side of Manhattan and got your name from the mailboxes in the lobby of your building.

Your name will not be used in the final dissertation. All interviews are anonymous and confidential. The topic of my dissertation is friendship patterns among urban single women.

Your cooperation will be greatly appreciated. In a few days I will follow up this letter with a phone call, requesting a time and place that we might meet to talk, at your convenience of course. Feel free to call me before that time at my home phone, listed below.

Sincerely yours,

Once permission to conduct the interview is granted—and if you are asking in person or over the phone, this may occur moments before you actually conduct the interview—you have to be prepared to schedule the interview or to carry it out immediately. It is generally expected that you are the one who should be inconvenienced the most in getting to the person you are interviewing, that, for example, the phone call will be on your telephone bill (especially if it is a long-distance call) and not theirs. Interviewing celebrities or very busy people, including anonymous interviewees whose opinions are crucial and not easily duplicated, requires razor-sharp decision making on your part as to time and place. Postponing an interview, whatever your reason, may mean never getting a second chance to do it. Be as accessible and as cooperative as possible. Until *you* are a celebrity, and perhaps even after that, you are beholden to those you interview far more than the reverse.

Conduct in-person interviews in segments of not more than two hours; if more time is needed, several interviews are better than one very long one. Phone interviews should be between twenty minutes and an hour; conduct several over a period of time if longer is needed. I recommend these short time spans for interviews because, unlike a relaxed conversation, an interview demands close attention and energy, yours and especially the interviewee's.

You will have to reveal some information about yourself to get the interview and some additional information to gain the interviewee's confidence and to help improve rapport, but everything you do and say during an interview is in the service of your role as a researcher. One of the most common mistakes made by untrained interviewers is talking too much. Whether it is done out of nervousness, or because interviewers are flattered that someone is interested in them, this is not only a time-waster but may actually be counterproductive. The interviewee may even encourage you to talk as an evasion tactic!

An interview is rigorous work. It requires planning on your part so that you know what you want to ask. Whether you are interviewing a celebrity or a scientist, to get the most out of an interview you'll have to do some background research about your topic or about the person you are interviewing.

Decide in advance what form of record keeping you will use—taking notes, using a tape recorder, or listening attentively and then writing furiously once you are finished with the interview. Tape recording permits you to have the greatest concentration during the actual interview. On rare occasions, an interviewee may object to the use of a tape recorder, or may be so inhibited by it that no interaction is possible, and then your only alternative will be to take notes or to memorize key phrases and write down as much as possible after the interview is over. If you choose to use a tape recorder, test out your machine before you arrive: At the beginning of the tape, record the name of the interviewee, the date, your topic, and play it back to check your machine. Begin the interview after that point. Take along an extra set of batteries. Unless your machine has an end alarm or cutoff switch, wear a watch to keep track of how much time you have left on any one side of your tape.

Taped interviews are records only of the verbal interaction; you may want to note nonverbal cues as well as physical details about the interviewee and the circumstances of the interview. To be most effective as a research tool, taped interviews should be transcribed, word for word, as soon after the interview as possible. A sample of a transcribed interview follows:

(Name, Address, and Phone Number of Interviewee)
Recorded—Tuesday, July 6, 1982 8:45–10:45 P.M.
Transcribed—Wednesday, July 7, 1982
(Introductory descriptive paragraph)
   JLB: Your age?
   SCJ: 32.

JLB: Place of birth?
SCJ: Brooklyn, New York.
JLB: Length of time you've been living in Manhattan?
SCJ: Seven years.
JLB: Education, how far did you go in school?
SCJ: I have an associate degree in nursing and I'm also a certified nurse practitioner.
JLB: And your occupation?
SCJ: Nurse practitioner.
JLB: Your marital status?
SCJ: Single.

Telephone interviews at least allow you to get some comments from persons who are too busy for an in-person interview or too far away, and they are fine for interviewing experts from whom you need just a brief quotation. Telephone interviews will save you time. However, for better or worse, phone interviews do not rely on the interactional rapport that may evolve during an in-person interview. You might use a telephone interview the way television producers do when they want to decide on a potential guest—as a pre-interview to be followed up by an in-person interview if desired.

As with in-person interviews, decide in advance how you will record the phone interview, whether by tape recording, taking notes, or listening carefully. If you decide to record the phone interview, there are ethical and legal considerations to be considered, and you should obtain permission from the person with whom you are speaking before you turn on your tape recorder. There are inexpensive devices you can buy to record directly from your telephone. (Note: The circular ones are better on standard phones than the suction cups, which may fall off.)

The most frequent reasons for poor in-person or telephone interviews are these:

On the part of the interviewer

1. Preparing inadequately.
2. Talking about yourself too much and not eliciting enough information from the interviewee.
3. Listening poorly during the interview so that you are pre-

vented from using the new information you have elicited
to direct the rest of the interview.

4. Allowing too little, or too much, time for the interview.
5. Failing to transcribe the interview immediately after-
wards, or to rewrite your notes.
6. Failing, out of shyness or laziness, to do follow-up interviews (if necessary).
7. Not checking quotations or having release forms signed,
(when appropriate).

On the part of the interviewee

1. Not allowing enough time for the interview.
2. Not being knowledgeable enough about the topic under
discussion but being reluctant to admit it.
3. Being a "problem" interviewee, such as a nontalker (inar-
ticulate), a compulsive talker, a pathological liar, or a
hostile, angry, or uncooperative person.
4. Permitting interruptions during the interview that interfere with the interaction.

To keep track of the interviews you conduct, evolve a
record-keeping system noting interviewees, times, places, circumstances, and summaries. One copy of the form on page 58 could
precede your taped transcript or notes and be filed chronologically; a second copy could be kept in a separate file, organized by
topic.

A final comment about interview etiquette: It is polite to
send a follow-up note, thanking interviewees for their time and
comments, whether or not you already have a signed release and
whether or not you plan to use the material. A secondary motive
is that your interviewee might be more willing to grant a second
or third interview, immediately or sometime in the future, if
you've been courteous and professional.

OBSERVATIONS

Another technique in gathering original research to
strengthen your writing is observation. Observation relies on what
you see as well as what you hear; the emphasis in interviewing is

INTERVIEW RECORD

Name: _____

Address: _____

_____

Phone: _____ (Home) _____ (Office)

Affiliation: _____

TOPIC OF INTERVIEW: _____

Date of interview: _____

Type: in-person telephone

Method of recording: tape notes other _____

Comments/observations: _____

_____

_____

_____

_____

Follow-ups:

Thank-you note sent No___ Yes___ Date_____

Release necessary   No___ Yes___

If yes, sent: Date_____

  Signed copy received: Date_____

Additional interviews:

Scheduled or completed:

Date: _____

on what you hear. There are two basic kinds of observers, insiders and outsiders. Insiders have a legitimate connection with the phenomenon under observation. The distinction rests on whether your intentions are known to your subjects. Let's say you are attending a Friday-night bingo game. As an insider, you write up what you hear and see and submit it to a newspaper as a first-person essay. By contrast, an outsider would go to a bingo game just to observe. (It might be appropriate, or necessary, to explain, and get cooperation, for your observation.) The excerpt that follows from George Orwell's book, *Down and Out in Paris and London*

(New York: Harcourt Brace Jovanovich, 1961) shows how observation helps a writer in uncovering the details and specifics that clarify and strengthen thoughts. The book is based on Orwell's experiences working as a dishwasher in a French restaurant. Note how concretely Orwell shows you the change in a waiter's behavior as he exits from the dirty kitchen into the luxurious dining room:

> As he passes the door a sudden change comes over him. The set of his shoulders alters; all the dirt and hurry and irritation have dropped off in an instant. He glides over the carpet, with a solemn priest-like air. I remember our assistant *maitre d'hôtel*, a fiery Italian, pausing at the dining-room door to address an apprentice who had broken a bottle of wine. Shaking his fist above his head he yelled (luckily the door was more or less soundproof):
>
> "*Tu me fais*—do you call yourself a waiter, you young bastard? You a waiter? You're not fit to scrub floors in the brothel your mother came from. *Marquereau!*"
>
> . . . Then he entered the dining-room and sailed across it dish in hand, graceful as a swan. Ten seconds later he was bowing reverently to a customer. And you could not help thinking, as you saw him bow and smile, with that benign smile of the trained waiter, that the customer was put to shame by having such an aristocrat to serve him.

Orwell's description of the waiter is effective writing because it not only conveys a definite thought but it is attentive to details that epitomize that thought, including the use of dialogue.

Julius A. Roth's *Timetables* provides another example of how observation aids writing. The author, a sociologist, researched as both an "insider" and an "outsider." He concealed the research purposes to which he put his initial hospital stay as a tuberculosis patient: "I did not confide my research interests or the fact that I was recording observations to any of the patients or staff. They observed me writing frequently, but assumed that I was pursuing my academic studies. In general, my relationship with other patients and with staff members was similar to that of most patients." Roth left that hospital for another; at the second hospital he did reveal his researcher's aim to one of the staff members. After his release, Roth obtained a grant and spent the next few years studying, and writing about, hospitals, this time as an outsider.

Here's another example of insider, or participant, observation. My assignment was to gather information about a hospital emergency room. I could have interviewed physicians, nurses, and patients; or I could have examined existing sources, accounts of emergency rooms written by hospital personnel, researchers, or writers. Instead, with the permission of the hospital administrator, I put on a white coat, became an unpaid clerk, and observed the emergency room as an insider. The staff members, but not the patients, were told that I was an observer. By performing the duties of a clerk, I was able to get an insider's view of an emergency room and also to be less conspicuous (and therefore a less inhibiting presence) than if I had stood around in street clothes taking copious notes.

We are all being observed and evaluated by others at work, in school, and in private situations. If these same experiences are viewed as research, however, you can apply disciplined and critical interpretations to what you see and hear and accumulate facts for your writing. Record your observations in your nonfiction writing notebook; it will serve as your field journal. Be sure to distinguish between what you observe and your interpretations of events. You will not be able to record everything; pay attention to what seems most important to you. If you already have a topic for your writing, the topic will help direct your attention. That topic or subject (whether "Employee Apathy in the Bank's Brazil Branch" or "Police–Community Relations in the Local Precinct") will help you to stay focused when you observe.

QUESTIONNAIRES AND SURVEYS

Suppose that a government employee without any statistical training is asked to devise a survey and to use it to collect data about her coworkers, or that a woman in a cultural affairs office needs to obtain information from theater owners on certain defined issues. Both of these workers decide that devising and distributing a written questionnaire is the best research method for their task. Both mail out questionnaires, analyze responses, and write out their reports. These are *self-administered* questionnaires in that the respondents answer the questions on their own. Surveys may be administered orally by a researcher; specific questions are asked and answered with the respondent in the researcher's presence. The researcher is assured of getting a completed questionnaire but cannot assure complete anonymity. Furthermore, the person whom you question may refuse to participate if you are asking at an inconvenient time; through the mail, the form may be completed more conveniently and confidentially.

In general, written questionnaires are less expensive, faster, and more anonymous than soliciting information in person or over the phone. When devising questions for your "self-administered" written survey, keep these guidelines in mind:

1. In a cover letter, or at the beginning of the survey, explain who you are, and why you are requesting this information.
2. State whether the respondent—the person answering the questionnaire—will be identified or anonymous.
3. Organize your questions as you would any writing task, namely by following some order, such as from broad to personal or from specific to general.
4. Ask questions that are clear and unambiguous.
5. Vary the form of your questions, and the possible answers, to keep the reader's interest high; include multiple choice, fill-in, and essay questions.
6. Pretest your questionnaire so that your final one is in the best form possible.
7. Unless absolutely necessary, avoid asking questions about income. Respondents will be more likely to describe their sexual activities than their financial affairs.

Conducting interviews, making observations, and distributing and analyzing questionnaires are time-consuming research methods. You might, therefore, use as your main research tool or as a supplement to your original work, facts and opinions that others have gathered. Here are some suggestions for using these kinds of materials.

USING EXISTING SOURCES

Existing sources may be primary, original research that someone else has compiled, such as audio or video tapes, diaries, autobiographies, and letters, or may be secondary sources in which information has been presented, analyzed, and interpreted by someone else, such as newspaper and magazine articles and books. Although extracting a quotation from an oral-history tape differs from excerpting a quotation from a secondary source, both kinds of existing sources may be regarded for your purposes as basic fact-finding research.

In *Finding Facts Fast* (New York: Morrow, 1972), veteran nonfiction writer Alden Todd, who teaches a course in fact finding in the School of Continuing Education of New York University, notes the multiple skills that a fact finder needs: "A first-class research worker needs techniques that combine the skills used by four kinds of professionals: the *reference librarian*, the *university scholar*, the *investigative reporter*, and *the detective. . . .* the excellent researcher should learn essential skills from each, and combine them so that they support one another."

To get the facts that will strengthen your nonfiction writing, learn how to find your way around libraries. If you feel as intimidated in a library as you might in a country where you cannot speak the language, brush up on how to use the library. Become as comfortable using the catalog cards as you probably feel looking something up in a telephone directory. Find out how to locate books on the shelf, or how to request them if your library does not have open stacks. Gain a working knowledge of standard reference books, and know where to find them: *The Harper Encyclopedia of Science, Cassell's Encyclopedia of World Literature, Encyclopedia of the Social Sciences, Encyclopaedia Britannica, Dictionary of American Biography,* and so forth. Enlist the aid of librarians, who are experts in research techniques and in the subjects of their particular collections, as you dig for information. I have sometimes found it productive to introduce myself to a librarian, explain my specific writing project, and develop a rapport so that I can call on him or her for future inquiries. In addition to the public library, learn about special libraries with collections geared to your topic. Become familiar with the various newspaper and magazine indexes such as *The New York Times Index* and the *Reader's Guide to Periodical Literature*, as well as with specialized ones, such as *Education Index, Applied Science & Technology Index, Social Sciences and Humanities Index*, and *Index to Legal Periodicals*. Learn how to locate entries to facilitate your research.

There are, of course, other ways of gaining access to existing sources than by using public libraries or special collections. Public-relations companies may be willing to provide you with research related to their clients' products or activities. Companies and television and radio stations may offer written materials, including transcripts, related to products or programs.

Here are some criteria for evaluating existing sources:

- Who is the author? What are his or her qualifications for writing this material?
- If the work is published, what kind of publisher, or periodical, published the material? What reputation does the company or publication have for checking out facts or having reliable authors?
- If the material is from a book, are there published reviews that you might consult to get other reactions to this work? As a test of excellence (or popularity), has this book been updated, revised, and issued in subsequent editions? Has this article been reprinted in collected works?
- If the research you are doing is in an area where new facts are calling into question previously written materials, does this work's date of publication or copyright rule it out as the best contemporary reference?
- Finally, what is your gut instinct about this material? If it is supposed to be objective, does its author seem to have an ax to grind? Or does the material seem to be a careful consideration of all sides of an issue?

You will need an orderly system of note taking if your research is to aid and not overwhelm your writing process. For bibliographic research, consider using the following card as a prototype of a system adapted to fit your needs. Have one card for each and every book, article, or report that you read. In the top blank area, note vital bibliographic information such as title, author, and details of publication. In the top right blank areas, write the major topic that this item refers to, as well as related topics for cross-indexing. (You may find it useful to jot down a library call number if you find the work in a library: This can save time if you need to consult the work again.)

(TOPIC):_____	
(LOCATION OF THIS MATERIAL)_____	
(AUTHOR):	
(TITLE):	
(PUBLISHER/PLACE & DATE OF PUBLICATION):	
SUMMARY:	
COMMENTS:	
COMPARED TO OTHER WORKS:	
ADDITIONAL NOTES: 1st reading_____ 2nd reading_____	

A sample of how a completed card might look follows:

Book Proposals
Editors
Filed under ''Getting Published''

Miner, Margaret
''What Editors Want in Book Proposals''
Authors Guild Bulletin, Summer 1983, pp.
3-4

SUMMARY: Based on interviews with top trade-
book editors, Miner lists 6 basic items that a
proposal should include, in addition to a cover
letter: 1) description of book 2) chapter outline 3) author's biography 4) information for
cost estimates 5) marketing information 6) sample chapter or two

---

COMMENTS: Who is this geared to, the new or
seasoned writer? Is the one or two sample-chap-
ter requirement that she suggests advantageous
whatever one's track record?

COMPARED TO OTHER WORKS: See Appelbaum and
Evans' *How to Get Happily Published*, pp. 82-5
and Neil Baldwin, ''Making the Decision to Publish,'' *Publishers Weekly* (3/23/84), pp. 18-21.

ADDITIONAL NOTES: Points #4, 5, and 6 are
especially worth noting.
1st reading 8/2/83   2nd reading 1/24/84

Now that you have something to write about, with ample research to back up your thoughts, you are ready to address yourself to stylistic concerns.

EXERCISES

1. Pick one possible writing idea and record it below:

   _____

   Now write one statement about the reason for this idea.
   Reason statement:_____
   Narrow down your reader or audience.
   Audience:_____
   Write one sentence clarifying the main thought to this writing idea.
   Main thought:_____
   Make an outline for developing this writing idea into a final written document.

2. Conduct an in-person or telephone interview about non-fiction writing with someone knowledgeable in this area.

3. Find a memo, report, letter, or any other example of your writing from the last year. Reread it, noting what kind of research you could have done, or examples you could have used, to have made your points more effectively.

4. Apply what you have learned about content to a current writing project or one you will have to, or want to, do in the near future. Create systems and procedures to try out on this new project. Decide on deadlines for the planning, research, writing, and rewriting phases of this writing task.

5. You want to write about ways to make better use of commuting time. List three approaches to this topic, including alternative research methods that you might follow.

REFERENCES

Barzun, Jacques. *On Writing, Editing, and Publishing.* Chicago: University of Chicago Press, 1971.

Barzun, Jacques and Henry E. Graff. *The Modern Researcher,* 3rd ed. New York: Harcourt Brace Jovanovich, Inc., 1977.

Emerson, Ralph Waldo. "Intellect," in *Emerson's Essays.* New York: Harper & Row, 1926, 1951.

Gross, Ronald. *The Independent Scholar's Handbook.* Reading, Massachusetts: Addison-Wesley, 1982. A thorough guide to how you can "make the joys of the intellect a significant part of your life" outside of traditional academia.

Lannon, John M. *The Writing Process.* Boston: Little, Brown and Company, 1983.

McCormick, Mona. *The New York Times Guide to Reference Materials.* New York: Popular Library, 1971. An annotated guide, with illustrated examples, of basic references books categorized by type, such as biographies or dictionaries, and by subject area, such as art, music, plays, and science.

Roth, Julius A. *Timetables.* Indianapolis: Bobbs-Merrill Company, Inc., 1963.

5

Style

A writer's style is his own distinctive way of expressing his personality in vocabulary, idiom, and sentence structure. Another man's style cannot be consciously copied without plagiarism. In fact, trying to imitate another's style is much the same thing as trying to disguise one's identity behind a papier-mâché mask that looks like Bernard Shaw or G.K. Chesterton. It might be amusing for a fancy dress ball, but only a lunatic would attempt to go about that way in ordinary life.
—*The Golden Book on Writing* by David Lambuth and others

Style is *how* you express the content of your writing. It is not only the words you choose but the way in which you link them together in sentences and paragraphs. Style includes punctuation, grammar, tone, length, and organization. There is a major difference between the stylistic issues that I will deal with and those that your college composition teachers might have stressed. This chapter is not a substitute for detailed discussions of grammar, or even a course in how to write a perfect sentence. Instead, it will alert you to the importance of writing simple, clear sentences and unified paragraphs that will help you to get your ideas across.

The poor writing of American students has been receiving a lot of attention, and rightly so: not just students in public high schools, junior or community colleges, but students at the more prestigious universities as well. "Every year, 40 to 60 percent of the students at the University of California find themselves required to enroll in remedial English," writes Christopher Lasch in *The Culture of Narcissism* (New York: Warner Books, 1979). "At Stanford, only a quarter of the students in the class entering in 1975 managed to pass the university's English placement test, even though these students had achieved high scores on the Scholastic Aptitude Test," Lasch continues.

Here are some stylistic errors gleaned from a few of my own college students:

Spelling errors: *alright* for *all right; quite* for *quiet; piers* for *peers; shuld* for *should; haven* for *having.*

Usage: using *a* before a word beginning with a vowel rather than *an* ("is *a* important"); confusing *to* with *too* or *hole* with *whole;* putting "in my opinion" within quotations marks; writing run-on sentences ("I just do the things I like to do, if that gets me publicity, fine.").

In response to the need to upgrade the writing of American students and company employees, writing is being taught differently today. Schools and corporations have started to bring in outside consultants—professional writers and writing teachers—to augment prior composition courses, which are often taught by people who majored in English literature rather than writing or education. The emphasis in these programs is on mastering good writing, not just on learning the infinite details of grammar.

Good nonfiction writing follows four basic principles:

- Correctness
- Readability
- Thought (discussed in Chapter 5)
- Appropriateness

These four principles are the basis of seminars that are being taught around the country. Barry Tarshis and Joanne Feierman have shared with me the programs that they teach in Connecticut and New York City, respectively. Tarshis, a journalist who also teaches nonfiction writing at Fairfield University, says, "I don't teach style. I teach readability. *Style* gets people into trouble. In business particularly, I always tell my students, 'Nobody takes a memo to read by the fire and nobody takes a report to read at the beach. They just want to get the information as fast and as quickly as they can.' The best style is a style that isn't noticed. I try to get most people to write as they speak."

Tarshis also detailed what he covers in his two-day writing seminar:

1. *How to write without pain,* which deals with the writing process.
2. *Reader sensitivity.* Learning the elements of writing that produce the kind of material seminar participants would themselves like to read, namely, short sentences, short paragraphs, conversational tone.
3. *Communicate with impact.* The words that you choose as well as details to back up your ideas.
4. *Sentence surgery.* In addition to emergency-room editing, you learn to accept what you have written as appropriate for the task at hand and that you will never have the "perfect" memo.

Joanne Feierman's company is Seminars in Communication. Feierman, who has both an M.A. in English and an M.B.A., has worked in industry and seen how good managers with poor writing skills often fail to get the attention and respect they deserve. Therefore, Ms. Feierman says, "I explain to my students and clients that the purpose of our work together is to make them look good on paper, to make them look as organized and as competent as they really are." To demonstrate to her participants how a well-written memo projects an image of professionalism, while a disorganized, long-winded one communicates the opposite image, Ms. Feierman asks participants to read poorly written and well-written versions of the same memos. They are then asked to describe how capable and intelligent they think the writers of the various memos are. Again and again, participants describe the authors of the well-written memos as being more competent and intelligent than the authors of the other memos—and this, of course, despite the fact that both versions contain the same ideas. Ms. Feierman then takes her participants through a series of writing exercises that show them how to write the good, clear, businesslike memos their careers demand.

As Feierman and other writing experts are quick to point out, the style of your nonfiction writing, as well as its format, depends on your audience, whether it is a memo, report, thesis, or magazine article. This chapter covers general principles of style; Chapter 6 applies those principles to specific kinds of writing tasks. However, before going on to a discussion of how correctness, readability, and appropriateness might be achieved in your writing, let's look at some short examples of nonfiction writing.

Recognizing good writing will help you to improve your own prose.

EXAMPLES OF EFFECTIVE WRITING

Example 1

Read this paragraph and then answer the questions that follow it:

> Although I have now rejoined all my friends and relatives, I wrote most of the text that follows this page during the twenty-six months that I lived by myself in the beautiful and breathtaking woods in a quaint house that I built all by myself. I was also self-employed during those twenty-six months, but certainly I made enough of an income by doing handiwork.

What's your first impression of the above paragraph—is it wordy or succinct? Is there just enough detail or too much? Does that paragraph make you want to read on, or to put down that writer's essay and go on to something else?

Now compare that paragraph to another version with the same ideas:

> When I wrote the following pages, or rather the bulk of them, I lived alone, in the woods, a mile from any neighbor, in a house which I had built myself, on the shore of Walden Pond, in Concord, Massachusetts, and earned my living by the labor of my hands only. I lived there two years and two months. At present I am a sojourner in civilized life again.

The second paragraph is the actual opening to one of the most famous first-person essays written by an American, Thoreau's *Walden*, published in 1854. Stylistically, it may seem to violate one of the rules suggested to you in the first chapter of this book (the first sentence has an abundance of commas by modern standards, though practice was different in Thoreau's day). However, compared to the first version that I wrote to illustrate a few points about ineffective writing, it is simpler, clearer, and more graceful, and it actually conveys *more* information.

Example 2

Examine this sentence for style:

Based on my vast travels and interviews as well as my observations, I have come to believe that Latins consider themselves
to be very good at making love (courtship, necking, petting, etc.)
and, by contrast, that Americans are perceived as vastly inferior to
them in the area of lovemaking.

Reexamine that sentence. Does it get the point across? Certainly. It is succinct and clear? Certainly not.
Now read this version:

You cannot spend an hour in the society of any Latin male
without hearing what bad lovers Americans are.

The second version is the last line from Helen Lawrenson's
controversial article, "Latins Are Lousy Lovers," which appeared
in the October 1936 issue of *Esquire* magazine. The strength of
her simple prose is clear when you compare her sentence to the
wordy version. Lawrenson's version has a lilt to it, a flow and tone
that makes you want to read more—to find out *why* she made her
opening statement. To achieve that simplicity and flow, however,
Lawrenson probably reworked that sentence numerous times.
The simpler and easier a sentence is to read, the more likely it
went through many revisions.

Example 3

This next example is a good illustration of how dialogue can
enliven your writing and convey your main points. Sally
Wendkos Olds' first-person essay appeared in *McCall's* magazine
and began in this way:

"Do You Want Your Mother to Die?"
"Yes," I say.
I have, of course, voiced the unspeakable, put into words
what no one should ever think, let alone admit, but my friend Jane
is not shocked. "So do I," she responds huskily. "Every time I call
my sister in St. Louis and ask, 'How's Mother?' and she says,
'Fine,' my heart sinks."

Jane's mother's heart still beats and her lungs still pulsate, but "fine" is a tragic misstatement of her condition. For the past year she has not recognized her daughters, has not known where she is or seemed to care.

Example 4

The next paragraph is from an article by Saul S. Radovsky, M.D., "Medical Writing: Another Look," which appeared in the July 19, 1979, issue of *The New England Journal of Medicine:*

Science makes for poor writing in a number of ways. Not only may skill in science select against skill in writing and busy scientists neglect how they write, but it also seems that as medical science advances, the quality of its writing declines.

Notice how Radovsky's first sentence informs the reader of the theme of the article. The opening sentence also tells the reader where Radovsky is going; the second part of the paragraph relates to the first, telling the reader *why* science makes for poor writing.

Example 5

The next paragraph is an example of simple sentences and words used to convey an important idea clearly. This paragraph is from *How to Read a Book* by Mortimer J. Adler and Charles Van Doren, first published in 1940 by Simon and Schuster:

If you ask a living teacher a question, he will probably answer you. If you are puzzled by what he says, you can save yourself the trouble of thinking by asking him what he means. If, however, you ask a book a question, *you must answer it yourself.* In this respect a book is like nature or the world. When you question it, it answers you only to the extent that you do the work of thinking and analysis yourself.

None of the above examples is as dependent on style as is the first sentence of Charles Dickens' *A Tale of Two Cities:* "It was the best of times, it was the worst of times." In these five examples, changing a word here or there would not drastically affect the final product. For now, avoid worrying about whether a sentence or two from your report, letter, or book is going to be quoted in the next edition of Bartlett's *Familiar Quotations*. It is sufficient if the style of your nonfiction writing sets forth your ideas clearly and with just enough detail to fit your particular audience.

PLAYING BY THE RULES (CORRECTNESS)

Correctness refers to the topics included in *grammar*, a Latin word defined by *Webster's* as "the study of the classes of words, their inflections, and their functions and relations in the sentence" (a definition that could certainly be clarified and simplified, as it was by Kesselman-Turkel and Peterson in *The Grammar Crammer* [Chicago: Contemporary Books, Inc., 1982], into "the study of the written word").

If you get upset when someone says "grammar," take comfort in the fact that grammar or correctness is only one element of good writing, albeit an important one if you do not want to appear illiterate. Improving your grammar will certainly help you to improve your writing; your self-confidence will grow as you master the basics of grammar. Consider taking a refresher course and, in the meantime, having your writing reviewed by someone who is expert in grammar.

Some aspects of grammar, however, such as correct spelling, are easy enough; just check the spelling of any words you are unsure about in a reliable dictionary. Of course, if you are sure of a misspelling, or if you correctly spell the wrong word, you have a problem of a different order. Punctuation is the next-easiest part of grammar to master; there are twelve symbols you should know, recognize, and properly use. Those symbols, from most commonly to least frequently used, are:

- Period
- Comma
- Question mark

- Colon
- Parentheses
- Dashes
- Underline
- Quotation marks
- Exclamation point
- Semicolon
- Brackets
- Ellipsis

If you are uncertain about any of the above punctuation marks, you will find explanations of what they are and how to use them in any high school or college composition text. A good short discussion of these punctuation marks, including examples of proper usage, is contained in Kesselman-Turkel and Peterson's *The Grammar Crammer.* You will also find it useful to consult the series of articles on punctuation by William A. Sabin, coauthor of *Reference Manual for Stenographers and Typists,* 4th edition (New York: McGraw Hill Book Company, Gregg Division, 1970), that appeared in *Business Education World* magazine from 1969–70. Each article is devoted to a single grammatical issue; two are concerned with specific punctuation marks—"The Semicolon; And Other Myths" and "The Comma Trauma."

But all the rules of correct English that you may vaguely recall from your schooldays present the most demanding aspect of correctness. A mere list of all the possible rules that you should know about has dubious value. I suggest that you write a sample paragraph or two off the top of your head and have it analyzed by a writing teacher or consultant for any glaring or consistent grammatical errors. Barring a course in usage, working on your specific grammatical problems (such as rules for adding an *s* to indicate a possessive noun or whether or not to use *who* or *whom*) is probably the best way to improve for your business, school, and personal writing needs. I'm not suggesting that you ignore the benefits of thoroughly mastering all the rules of usage. I'm simply suggesting it may be impractical to expect yourself to do that. Therefore, with grammar as with spelling, when in doubt, look it up. Have on hand one or more grammar texts for reference. If your company has a communications department that will read over finished manuscripts for correctness, take advantage of it for expert suggestions. If necessary, hire an outside editor to correct your writing. Publishers do this all the time for their professional writers; it's called copy editing. It's ethical, legitimate, and even expected that you have someone who *is* an expert in grammar give a finished manuscript a once-over.

The two little books that John Fielden (see page 46) recommends for refreshing you on correctness are Strunk and White's *The Elements of Style,* already mentioned in the first chapter of this book, and David Lambuth's *The Golden Book of Writing* (New York: Penguin Books, 1964). Like *The Elements of Style, The Golden Book of Writing* evolved out of lectures delivered by an English professor, David Lambuth, who taught at Dartmouth College, where his *Golden Book* was first published in 1923. Lambuth's book, which was written in collaboration with four other English teachers (K.A. Robinson. H.E. Joyce, W.B. Pressey, and A.A. Raven), is a succinct yet comprehensive rulebook for correct writing. Like *Elements of Style,* it covers all the essentials of good writing, including punctuation, usage, the sentence, the paragraph, and organizing the whole piece of writing.

To facilitate writing correctly, make yourself a style sheet. Magazines and book publishers often do this for their authors. If professionals who are supposed to know correctness have style sheets, think of how useful a customized style guide would be to you. One national magazine has a style sheet of some thirty rules, each one illustrated with a correct and an incorrect example. These rules are based on Strunk and White's *Elements of Style.* One book publisher distributes a house style sheet to its authors; spelling, grammar, and punctuation guidelines are based on *The Chicago Manual of Style.*

For your own style sheet, divide your page into two columns. On the left side, list the correct spelling of the words that you commonly misspell or that you are unsure about the correct form of (one word or two, hyphenated or not, etc.). On the right side, list any grammatical or usage problems that you typically make, such as confusing *who* with *whom, it's* with *its,* or *effect* with *affect.* Consult Strunk and White, Lambuth, or another good stylebook to create your mini style sheet. Here is a much-abbreviated version of the style sheet I created while writing this book:

STYLE SHEET

Spelling	Grammar
writer's block	*affect* is the verb; *effect*
legwork	is the noun
burnout	a speaker *implies*; a
percent	listener *infers*
nonfiction	J. T. Stevens *not* J.T. Stevens

Bibliographic Style

Bibliographic material at the end of each chapter conforms to the style suggested in *Words Into Type*, 3rd ed. (Englewood Cliffs, New Jersey: Prentice-Hall, Inc., 1974).

CLARITY (READABILITY)

Rudolf Flesch, among others, has codified what easy-to-read writing should look like. These are the elements:

- Short words
- Short sentences
- Short paragraphs

Your first concern in improving the readability of your nonfiction writing is to choose the right word. Your writing should use words most closely conveying the meaning of your thoughts. Flowery words and jargon should be avoided, if possible. Say what you have to say simply and clearly. If you want to say something is *elastic* or *buoyant* it is ostentatious to use *supernatant*. *Face* is clearer than *visage* or *countenance*. *Fade* is simpler than *achromatize*. In "Polluting Our Language," an article published in the Spring 1972 *American Scholar*, English professor Douglas Bush points out some of the kinds of jargon and wordy writing that you should avoid:

> There is the simple jargon of pretentious padding, sometimes pseudo-technical; no one ever teaches in college but always "at the college level"; a crow is not black but basically or essentially black; nothing happens before anything else but always "prior to." No one feels pleasure or anxiety or fear; he feels a sense of pleasure, a sense of anxiety, a sense of fear. A politician doesn't say "Yes"

but—if he is relatively forthright—"My answer is in the affirmative."

Just as simple words will aid your writing, simple sentences are easier to read. Generally, more than twenty words in a sentence make reading harder. You might also edit your paragraphs so they consist of four to eight sentences; one main idea to a paragraph will increase readability. Readability also includes the appearance of your writing. Twenty-sentence paragraphs, single-spaced manuscripts (double-spacing is easier on the eyes), and too-narrow margins at the top, bottom, or sides are physical aspects of writing that will affect readability.

In *On Writing Well,* teacher, writer, and editor William Zinsser emphasizes the importance of clarity in nonfiction writing:

> The writer must therefore constantly ask himself: What am I trying to say? Surprisingly often, he doesn't know. Then he must look at what he has written and ask: Have I said it? Is it clear to someone encountering the subject for the first time? If it's not, it is because some fuzz has worked its way into the machinery. The clear writer is a person clear-headed enough to see this stuff for what it is: fuzz. . . .
>
> Writing is hard work. A clear sentence is no accident. Very few sentences come out right the first time, or the third. Keep thinking and rewriting until you say what you want to say.

To achieve clarity in your writing you have to be clear and organized about what you want to write. Organization is a key to effective nonfiction writing. No doubt you have been creating bibliographic cards and notes on the original and secondary research related to your idea or topic. Ideally, you should be taking notes all along in this writing process—from idea to finished product—on what you want to say ultimately. These along-the-way notes will facilitate the way you will organize all your material, by clarifying the most important information to include in your first draft. For shorter writing projects, I simply jot down a list of points I want to cover, reordering as needed. I prefer to create a formal outline for longer nonfiction assignments. Some teachers, like management professor John S. Fielden, believe an outline to be a must, even before an executive dictates a report or memo. In "What Do You Mean I Can't Write?" Fielden notes: "... Most writers tend to think as they write; in fact, most of us do not even know what it is we think until we have actually written it down. The inescapability of making a well-thought-out outline before dictating seems obvious."

You may be writing notes and drafts as you pursue your research; you may prefer to delay writing anything until all your facts are in. You may prefer to write continually, adding pieces of information as they fit your overall research/writing plan. How you decide to proceed may be based on personal preference, considered judgment, or simply old habits from school, when you rushed to write that term paper the night before it was due. Ask yourself whether waiting till the bitter end to write up your research stems from a version of writer's block—you hate writing so you put it off till the last minute.

There are, however, two obvious reasons why writing at the last minute is ill-advised. The first reason is that waiting to write till all the research is in limits the time you have to spend on writing and improving the style of your project. The second reason is that the less time you allow for writing and rewriting, the less likely you are to make use of the learning experience that writing provides. The synthesis of your research may, alas, only occur as you look over what you have learned, take notes on key points, decide what material you will use to support your views, and do a first draft in your own words and style. Of course, the writing phase—when the research is behind you—can be lonely. The people you have interviewed, the places you have visited, the books you have read no longer distract you. It is just you and your typewriter (or word processor). Until you really get going and become absorbed in the magical writing process, the time may seem to drag and gnaw at you. Stay with it, however, and you will be transported to another sphere, tapping levels of your senses you rarely otherwise use.

So you have mountains of paper with notes or research on them. How do you put it all together to create a cohesive piece of writing? Here are a few steps to help you get organized before writing your first draft:

Step One: Make a list of key points or an outline for your writing. Look over the cards, notes, or materials you have amassed. Write one line to summarize each example, piece of research, or thought. Put one point on one index card, or make a list of points.

Step Two: Shuffle every point around, grouping together those points to be covered in the beginning, middle, or end of your first draft. You could put the cards into stacks labeled 1 (for beginning), 2 (for middle), and 3 (for ending); or you could write a number next to each item and then rewrite your summary statements so you have three separate lists.

Step Three: Remind yourself who you are writing this for—your audience. Your audience may help you to determine your organizing principles. A report to your employer about the conference he sent you to may begin with different facts than a report to coworkers who are considering attending a similar conference.

Step Four: Find an organizing principle for each section of your writing. Here are some principles you might consider:

- General to specific
- Specific to general
- Chronological order
- Thematic
- Cause and effect
    Effects backed up by cause
    Cause followed up by effects
- Compare and contrast
- Natural divisions evolved from your material
- The questions of "who," "what," "where," "when," "why," and "how"

In *Write for Results* (Boston: Little, Brown and Company, 1982), coauthors William D. Andrews and Deborah C. Andrews suggest these organizing principles:

- *Natural order,* imposed by the material
- *Logical order,* imposed by the writer
- *Psychological order,* imposed by the reader

You will apply these organizing principles to each paragraph as well as to the overall organization of the entire piece of writing.

Another consideration in organizing your material is what to put in and what to leave out. You have your overall organization, the main points you want to make, the sequence in which your ideas will be presented. Now you need to decide what examples or facts you will use, and which ones you will discard, to best support your points. Once again, your audience may help you in your determinations, as well as structural considerations such as length. An essay on success in *Vogue* would be backed up by different examples from one on the same subject for *The Nation* or *The Gerontologist.*

With your facts and notes assembled before you, reordered within your organizing principle, your next step is to write your first draft. I recommend freewriting it with little attention to style. You can attend to the style in subsequent drafts. *Get it all down* is the most important step to take at this point. Fill in the structure you have created. Write the draft that you will mold until it best conforms to your thoughts and expectations for this writing task.

Now that you have your first draft, read it over from beginning to end, checking its organization. Put it aside for a day or two and come back to it with a fresh eye. Show it to someone whose opinions you trust to get feedback. Reread your first draft and ask yourself if each statement has enough supporting data—examples, illustrations, quotations—to back it up. Is paragraph 1 where it should be, or might it be better to move it to the middle of your writing?

Clarifying what you say means applying organizational considerations to *every draft of your writing.* You organize *before* you write and then, upon reading your first draft, you *reorganize* each successive draft until you are pleased with your final draft. It is after the first-draft stage that the cut-and-paste part of writing occurs. Whether you physically cut and paste, or whether you do it electronically on your word processor, reorganizing will make your writing clearer, more professional, and easier to read and understand. Material you realize should be added is indicated with an insert and attached to your manuscript, or actually added in at the appropriate place. (Retyping will eliminate all the inserts or indications that anything was cut and pasted.) Material that you decide to eliminate in subsequent drafts is deleted.

READER APPEAL
(APPROPRIATENESS)

Nothing is written in a vacuum. A personal diary entry, intended only for the author's catharsis and not for other eyes, is usually more open, honest, and self-examining than a report to an employer of that same day's activities would be. Appropriateness has to do with the kind of writing you are doing as well as the audience for your writing. Consider the business or personal letters you have received recently. Was the amount of detail appropriate to the kind of writing, or was there too much or too little? Too little detail makes writing seem impersonal and abrupt; too much detail wastes the reader's time on irrelevancies.

Appropriateness also refers to tone, which is, once again, dependent on the kind of writing and the audience. Even the decision of whether or not to use footnotes, and the form and style of those footnotes, will be affected by the audience for whom you are writing. As London *Times* literary editor and wordsmith Philip Howard writes in his collection of columns, *Words Fail Me* (New York: Oxford University Press, 1981): "Each of us uses many different dialects of English." The dialect of a memo may be inappropriate for a technical article; the dialect of a goodwill business letter may be inappropriate for the annual report.

EXERCISES

1. The sentence that follows (taken from a student's composition) has one asset—it's short—but it is still an example of poor writing:

   Rethinking pollution will save our finite ecosystem.

   Rewrite the above sentence according to the guidelines you have learned for effective writing.

2. Read the following letter to a colleague, keeping in mind John Fielden's four principles of good writing: correct-

ness, readability, thought, and appropriateness. What improvements could have been made in a second or third draft? Does the nature of this writing task justify revisions?

September 5, 1983

Dear ———,

If you haven't yet filled out your first questionnaire, I'm enclosing a second one that is slightly improved. I'm trying to get at least 100 responses so I'd appreciate your answers and/or giving this to another writer that you know.
Thanks!

All my best,

Would indented paragraphs have made the above letter more readable? Does it make its points clearly and succinctly?

3. Correct the punctuation in the following paragraph:

Every would be professional writer dreams of breaking in with that juicy cover story for McCall's that of course is reprinted in Readers' Digest? Then its just a matter of selecting from the steady flow of assignments as each completed article is accepted praised bought and promptly published Now that youre awake we can probably agree that except for the instant success stories that usually prove to be more fiction than fact building a literary career is often a question of submissions rejections and eventually acceptances.

4. You want to write a book chapter on getting organized for a general audience. How would you order the points that follow so everything could be included in a logical, organized way?

Organizing a desk
Creating a filing system
Organizing a bookcase
Distinguishing priorities from busywork
Organizing a day
Improving decision making

5. What is the organizing principle behind the first two paragraphs of this essay, excerpted from William Gilman's *The Language of Science: A Guide to Effective Writing* (New York: Harcourt, 1961):

> We are all guilty, more or less, of writing jargon. We are all guilty, too, of complaining about other people's jargon while we tolerate it in our own writing. Sometimes it sneaks past our guard. Other times we drag it in to brandish our knowledge—or hide what we don't know.
>
> ... *Metals Progress* magazine offers these examples of the kinds of statements that occur in research reports, and in parentheses explains what they really mean:
>
> While it has not been possible to provide definite answers to these questions ... (The experiment didn't work out, but I figured I could at least get a publication out of it.) ...
>
> Correct within an order of magnitude. (Wrong)

Can you think of other ways to have organized this material?

6. Return to the freewrite you did for exercise 2 at the end of Chapter 2 in this book. Rewrite that freewrite, keeping in mind all the stylistic issues raised in this chapter, including correct spelling, punctuation, word usage, short sentences and paragraphs, and clear, organized thoughts.

REFERENCES

Baker, Sheridan. *The Practical Stylist With Readings,* 5th ed. New York: Harper & Row, 1982. Although geared to writing the undergraduate English composition, Baker's book covers basics of good writing with ample examples.

Barnet, Sylvan, and Marcia Stubbs. *Barnet & Stubbs's Practical Guide to Writing,* 4th ed. Boston: Little, Brown and Company, 1983. Sound advice and examples in this basic college text, useful to anyone who must do expository writing.

Flesch, Rudolf. *How to Say What You Mean in Plain English.* New York: Barnes & Noble Books, 1972.

Maeroff, Gene I. "Teaching of Writing Gets New Push," *The New York Times* (January 8, 1984), Section 12, pp. 1, 36.

Postman, Neil, Charles Weingartner, and Terence P. Moran. eds. *Language in America.* New York: Western Publishing Company, Inc., 1969. Collection of essays covering such wide-ranging areas of language as advertising, education, love, censorship, and racism.

Reed, Sally. "Schools Put Creative Writers to Work," *The New York Times* (January 8, 1984), Section 12, pp. 42–3.

Simmons, Nicole. "Writing Spreads Across the Curriculum," *The New York Times* (January 8, 1984), Section 12, pp. 36–7.

Strunk, William, Jr., and E.B. White. *The Elements of Style,* 2nd ed. New York: Macmillan, 1972.

Zinsser, William. *On Writing Well,* 2nd ed. New York: Harper & Row, 1980.

6

Writing for Work, School, or Personal Reasons

Have you received informative letters with the appropriate conversational tone, to-the-point memos, or well-written and organized reports? Have you ever written a term paper for school that you actually wanted to reread after your teacher graded and returned it? Whether or not you aspire to becoming a full-time professional writer, you can probably think of numerous occasions in your work, school, or personal life when being able to write effectively is an advantage. Business writing that is too bland can be as damaging to your career as writing that is too flamboyant. The key to personal or business writing that aids communication and advances your image in the eyes of its readers is to be true to yourself—but in the service of the role that you are playing. Are you writing in your role of devoted spouse? dutiful employee? provocative researcher? concerned citizen? probing student? annoyed customer?

Writing presents challenges that are missing when you speak. When you communicate verbally, you are usually speaking to a known audience, whether it consists of one or two other persons, a small group, or a large gathering. When you write, however, you are sometimes unsure whether what you write will be read by just one other person, or by many others. Furthermore, written communications are a concrete record of your thoughts and writing style, a fact that can cause you to block or inspire you to eloquence. A bank executive I interviewed, for example, believes it is a fear of writing poorly that causes many people to avoid doing it. "You tend to be judged by commission, rather than omission," she explains. True or not, there are some writing tasks that you have to do; in those cases, inaction constitutes an action.

Guidelines for becoming an effective written communicator parallel those for developing better verbal skills, as they have been outlined by Mark L. Knapp in *Social Intercourse: From Greeting to Goodbye* (Boston: Allyn & Bacon, Inc., 1978. My comments are in brackets).

- Knowledge [developing a sizable knowledge base]
- Experiences [practice]
- Motivation [wanting to improve]
- Attitudes ["increasing security in our identities"]

Keep those guidelines in mind as you learn tips and rules for specific kinds of writing.

LETTERS

"For most people letter writing is one case in which it is far better to receive than give," state N.H. and S.K. Mager in *The Complete Letter Writer*. Most of us would agree, although there are times you really want to write a letter, and (more frequently) times when you simply must write letters. Most of us have written letters we wish we had not mailed, but we have also sent, or received, letters that have meant a lot to us. Unlike the quick phone call (still a welcome form of communication), letters require an extra effort. They can be a keepsake. Receiving an eloquent letter can make your day; however, poorly written or tactless letters can hamper, or even end, your job or relationship. Being praised for a well-written letter is a high compliment.

Here are general guidelines for writing letters:

1. Let the purpose and audience for your letter determine its tone—formal or conversational for business letters; conversational and casual for personal.
2. Make the letter visually appealing and easy to read.
3. Write, edit, and rewrite all but the most personal stream-of-consciousness letters. Letters, like any writing that you do, are examples of your writing ability.
4. Generally, the shorter the letter, the better.
5. Avoid trite expressions, like "How are you? I'm fine" or "I'm writing in response to your letter of. . . ."

6. Letters offer you an opportunity to express your personality with the kind of paper you choose as well as with the words that you write. Select your letterhead or stationery with care.

7. Generally, letters should be answered promptly. Too long a delay in responding to a written communication is as impolite as failure to return phone calls immediately.

8. Avoid form letters, such as photocopied letters at Christmastime. A brief personal note, even handwritten, will be appreciated more than a lengthy form letter. In business matters, a short paragraph to a specific individual may be more effective than a long form letter to just anyone.

9. If possible, schedule time for letter writing separate from the time you devote to other kinds of writing, such as reports, magazine articles, or book proposals. The thought and creative effort that writing letters requires means less time and stamina for other demanding writing tasks. I am trying for a better solution, to be sure, but in the last few years I have found that I have to put aside nonpriority letter writing when I am in the heat of a writing project such as finishing the final draft of a book.

Personal Letters

"Reading your letter was like having company in the house," says an eighty-year-old widow. Personal letters can be the poems written by those only comfortable with prose. Personal letter writing is, unfortunately, becoming a lost art. Yet personal letters are valuable to the writer and recipient alike, even if only a few are exchanged in a year.

All kinds of occasions warrant sending a letter, even if your family and friends live in the same town or home. We send letters of congratulations and regret, thank-yous, love letters, and letters that share good news. Letters offer the opportunity to work out and rework your thoughts without interruption. If personal letters are used as a supplement to, not a replacement for, telephone and in-person communication, letters are a valuable way to express sensitive or delicate thoughts and feelings. "Despite my nonverbal reaction," a shy man writes to his beloved, "I am glad that you told me how you were feeling." Expressing thoughts he would have found extremely difficult to say, he continues writing,

"It reminded me of a truism: that we must strive each day to give each other the emotional support we need."

Be aware that although you may write a personal letter in a spare moment at your own convenience, your letter may arrive at a time that is particularly busy or inconvenient for your correspondent. Try to be as patient about someone reading and replying to your letter as you should be about phone calls that are received at an inopportune time.

Generally, the writer, not the receiver, is considered to be the "owner of copyright" on a letter.

Business Letters

Of course, there are numerous reasons for sending business letters. Among the most common ones are soliciting business or a new client; following up a phone call, interview, or transaction; making miscellaneous inquiries about such matters as job possibilities or product information; dealing with financial matters. Since business letters are usually written on letterhead, which includes your address, the heading of the letter often only requires the date. The rest of the letter includes the inside address (the person to whom you are writing), the salutation followed by a colon ("Dear Mr. Jones:"), the body of the letter, the closing ("Yours truly," "Sincerely yours," etc.), and your signature above the typed version of your name and your title. Letters that are typed by someone else customarily include the initials of the letter writer followed by the initials of the typist. The writer's initials are uppercase; the typist's, lowercase. If a copy of your letter is going to anyone else, it is traditional to note that with *cc:* followed by the name of the recipients of your copies. (This goes under your initials.) Since so many letters are now photocopied, rather than carbon copied, it has recently been suggested that you substitute "copy to:" or "copies to:".

The guidelines for effective business letters are the same as those for any kind of nonfiction writing: your letter should be correct, easy to read, well thought out, and appropriate in tone and content for its reader. Your letter should be organized with a beginning, a middle, and an end, and your reader should finish it with a clear idea of any action that should be taken.

The following sentence is the beginning of a letter written to an administrator; it could be called a goodwill letter in that it is optional but certainly appreciated by its recipient:

Dear ——:

Before any more time passes, let me thank you for allowing me to be a participant observer in the emergency room last month. . . .

Sincerely yours,

The letter above is an example of a block-style letter; an indented letter, this one an example of a letter soliciting new business, follows. Notice that the letter is short, simple, and clear—yet there is some originality to it, and you sense the writer's personality is reflected in its content:

Dear ——:

My colleague and mentor, ——, suggested I write to you regarding the possibility of —— having need for my professional skills and expertise. I am, therefore, pleased to attach a résumé for your perusal.

I look forward to hearing from you, at your convenience, and, I hope, to meet with you in the near future.

Sincerely yours,

Here's an example of a clear business letter written to fulfill a request for information:

Dear ——:

Enclosed is our catalogue and information on —— as you requested. We would be glad to arrange a screening of this film and any others you think would be suitable. Just give me or —— a call.

Sincerely yours,

encl.

There is a distinction between sending out a form letter and creating prototypes for typical letters to facilitate correspondence as situations arise. Creating prototypes is an excellent way of improving your letter-writing skills; knowing you will reuse a format may inspire you to expend extra effort on writing a sample for adaptation. Consider, for example, this sample format for thanking someone for a job inquiry:

Date

Inside name and address

Dear ———:

Thank you for your recent letter in response to my inquiry about a position at ———. I appreciate the time you took to reply personally.

Please keep me in mind if a position opens up that might be mutually beneficial.

Sincerely yours,

With business letters, as with reports, essays, or books, make a plan of what you want to write—your message—and try writing an idea-statement around which you can shape the rest of your letter. Ask yourself the same questions about the business letters you write that you should ask about all your writing, "Is this necessary writing?" "Do I have something to say that the reader wants to, or needs to, hear?" Numerous successful professionals and business people I have interviewed stressed that they have become more discriminating about whose phone calls they return, as well as about which letters they answer. If you think a business letter is called for, decide what you want to say and organize your letter as you would any other piece of writing. Type (or dictate) a first draft. Edit and revise. Retype, reread the finished version, sign it, and send it. Have a simple and dependable system for retrieving copies of correspondence—correspondence that you write as well as receive—and you will cut down on your overall research (searching) and even writing time.

If you want to communicate with someone within your company, it is usually more efficient to send them a memo than a formal business letter.

MEMOS

> Tom Wolfe, totally blocked on his first famous article, a story about customized cars for *Esquire*, wrote a really socko memorandum for his editor on the subject. The editor ran the memo as the article. Wolfe now writes all his articles as memos.
> —Reprinted from *Time*, October 3, 1977,
> in *Overcoming Writing Blocks* by Mack and Skjei

Your memos may never be published, but you may aid (or hamper) your career depending on what thoughts and writing abilities you demonstrate in them. A memo in business is, after all, similar to a note you might write in your personal life. In both cases, you probably want to put your best self forward. Also, both communications tend to focus on one specific item of information: paid vacation days for the coming year, congratulations on a glowing speech, scheduling the next staff meeting, the information you will convey in a story. Unlike the more formal business letter, memos allow you to get right to the point without appearing abrupt or curt (though you should investigate any company practice about the ideal tone for your memos).

If possible, keep your memos down to one page as well as confining them to one theme. If supporting materials are necessary, or if the readers of your memo are to fill something out and return it to you, attach such material, figures, tables, survey, or the like, to your memo. A lawyer who has worked in a variety of corporate and government settings tells me that she has discovered that the most effective memos are those that provide information by stating the writer's conclusions at the very beginning of the memo—grabbing the reader's attention and rewarding the reader for taking the time to read the memo—followed by the details of how the conclusions were reached.

Memos should be dated. Clearly indicate at the top to whom the memo is addressed, and follow this immediately with the subject of the memo. Memo paper facilitates observance of these guidelines. Most companies have a stock of prepared memo forms for the use of employees that follow this format:

Name of Company

Date:

To:

From:

Subject:

A well-written memo needs to adhere to the same rules of good writing that have been stressed throughout this book, namely, clarity of thought, simplicity of language, a definite idea of the audience, and logical organization. In most companies there are "political" considerations about the specific audience one wants for any particular memo. If you send your memo to everyone, it loses its impact. If you send it to persons too high or too low on the ladder, your status at the company can be altered and you risk being viewed as trying to ingratiate yourself inappropriately with either group.

Make your memos as visually pleasing and as easy to read as any other piece of writing by using short sentences and paragraphs, headings, and lists and steps instead of lengthy descriptions. If you are requesting the reader or readers to take some action on your memo, end your memo with that request, making sure your expectation is clear.

A model memo follows. Notice how it adheres to the above guidelines by providing all necessary details ("to," "from," "date," and "subject") at the very top, being short and to the point, simply written, appealing to the reader visually, ending with a request for action, and attaching supporting documentation.

MEMORANDUM

DATE: September 26, 1983
TO: Director and All Faculty
FROM: Drs. Lynn Levitt and Penny Haile
SUBJECT: UP FRONT: THE HUMAN RESOURCES DE-
VELOPMENT CENTER NEWSLETTER

The Winter issue of *Up Front: The Human
Resources Development Center Newsletter* is
expected to be published in January or
February of 1984. In order to update our
''Faculty News'' section, we would appreciate it if you could take a few moments
of your time to let us know what professional activities you have been involved
in this past spring and summer or are currently involved in. We have provided the
following form for your convenience.
    PLEASE COMPLETE THIS FORM AND PUT IT IN
THE MAILBOX OF LYNN LEVITT BY *MONDAY, OC-
TOBER 10th.*
    THANK YOU FOR YOUR COOPERATION.

REPORTS

You may be required to write reports in a variety of business
and school situations; your report may be circulated within your
company or school, or to outsiders as well. A report is basically a
written description of what you know, have found out, or have
done. In order to attract your reader's attention—most will as-
sume your report is another boring, poorly written, and overlong
document for them to wade through—begin with a catchy

phrase, a striking quotation, or an enticing conclusion lifted from your summary to hook your reader into continuing to read your report. Three among many possible openers are (1) a rhetorical question, such as, "Should the audit department be phased out by next year?"; (2) a provocative summary statement, such as, "The marketing department predicts our home computer will outsell our leading competitor's by next February"; and (3) an anecdote, quotation, or headline, such as " 'Staggered work hours to be in place by 1986,' Senior Vice-President reassures account executives."

When writing your report, be as succinct as possible; your employer or teacher will appreciate having to spend less time and effort on reading your document. Enliven your report with quotations (short and to the point), break up the text with titles and subheads that highlight key findings, and illustrate it with tables, graphs, or charts whenever possible.

Vincent Vinci, Director of Public Relations for Lockheed Electronics, cites the following report-writing problems in his article "Ten Report Writing Pitfalls: How to Avoid Them," which appeared in *Chemical Engineering*, December 22, 1975:

1. Ignoring your audience
2. Writing to impress
3. Having more than one aim
4. Being inconsistent
5. Overqualifying
6. Not defining
7. Misintroducing
8. Dazzling with data
9. Not highlighting
10. Not rewriting

When I was the coordinator of the Community Crime-Prevention Resource Center housed at Marymount Manhattan College's library, I had to write a monthly progress report. Each report detailed my accomplishments during the previous month. (This approach differs from a proposal in that a proposal states what you intend to do. In the next chapter, for example, an example of a book proposal is presented and discussed.) The first question I had to ask (and answer) to write my report was one you are no doubt familiar with by now, "Who is this report's audience?" Next, I needed an organizing principle for the information that I presented. To condense vast information, and to maintain reader interest, consider employing an organizing principle other than straight chronological order. You might instead organize your information by major points or theses, backing them up by examples or details. My monthly reports, for example, were organized around themes that reflected the emphasis that month, with heads or descriptive phrases set off from the text to highlight the themes. These themes included Publicity Activities, Community Use of the Resource Center, and New Acquisitions. You should also consider organizing some or all of your numerical data into charts or tables, which are clearer and more readable than statistic-laden prose. For example, I included in each report a summary of the acquisitions for my Center, presenting that information in a simple chart:

MARCH ACQUISITIONS

Kind of Material	Number
Books	25
Journals	4
Magazine articles	75
Miscellaneous materials (200):	
Descriptive brochures	90
Letters	80
Films	5
Tapes	25
Total	304

If I had presented the same information in the body of my report, it would have been quite tedious for the reader to follow, and the facts would have been obscured.

Ron S. Blicq's *Guidelines for Report Writers* spells out his "pyramid" approach to report writing. The pyramid method means that the report's main message is presented right up front, on top, followed by a base of supporting information, facts, and details. This organizational style is, in effect, the same as has already been advocated for memos. Since reports are longer and more complicated than memos, however, adhering to the pyramid principle will take you far toward improving readability.

In summary, when writing a report, apply the following questions to that task:

1. Who will read this report?
2. What is my purpose in writing it?
3. What is the main point I have to make?
4. What details will I use to back up my major conclusion?
5. Will I make any recommendations at the conclusion of this report?
6. Should I include an abstract summarizing my findings, so that readers can decide whether they need to read more or so that they will have a clear statement of my major conclusions?
7. What format, if any, should I follow for quoted material or bibliographic references?

Set a deadline for the first draft of your report, allowing at least as much time for rewriting as for doing your initial draft. Since several years of work for a company, or a large percentage of your course grade, may be based on just one report, make sure your final document is lively, clear, organized, and so well written that it will be both read and praised.

EXAMS, PAPERS, THESES, AND DISSERTATIONS

The most important writing advice to keep in mind for school-related writing is to consider your audience and to be clear about deadlines (how much time you have to complete an essay, a term paper, a thesis, or a dissertation). All school-related writing is pressure writing, which may cause you either to panic or to feel challenged. By failing to budget your time, you increase the likelihood of a panic response. "I was rushed at the end of my allotted time," writes a seventeen-year-old student who experienced writer's block during an essay examination.

Clarify what your audience—teacher or school—requires for

any particular assignment. Usually your teacher or school will advise you as to length and format and perhaps even about acceptable writing ideas or topics.

All previous suggestions for effective nonfiction writing apply in school settings, although your reports will probably rely more on library research than would, say, a business report, which would probably stress what you have actually done. Apply the rules of all good writing to school reports: clarity, organization, enough detail to back up your statements, appropriateness to your audience, and correct spelling, punctuation, and grammar.

If you freeze up on essay exams, you are experiencing a version of writer's block. Review the causes and cures of writer's block discussed in Chapter 2. When you take an essay exam, after you read each exam question, ask yourself this rhetorical question, "What do I want to say?" Budget enough time to answer each essay question completely. Simply take the total number of questions, divide it by the time allotted for your test, and give yourself *x* number of minutes for writing each answer. If you finish a question faster, so much the better. If you are permitted to make notes during a test, rough out a list of points to be covered in each answer, and write your answer with a beginning, middle, and end, as you would for any nonfiction writing task.

For term papers that require research, pick a topic that is as narrow as possible. If your teacher expects six to ten typed, double-spaced pages, you would probably be able to do a more interesting and complete job on "The Nun in Chaucer's *Canterbury Tales*," than on "Old English Poets"; "The Effect of Separation on Five-Year-Olds" is more likely to produce a cogent essay than "Children and Divorce." In writing up your report, make sure you consult, and follow, a recommended bibliographic and footnote style, such as Kate L. Turabian's *A Manual for Writers of Term Papers, Theses, and Dissertations.* Even if your term paper is for chemistry or physics, carefully check the spelling and grammar of your final draft. Rewrite and retype any school report or take-home examination so that you hand in perfect copy. Avoid obscuring your ideas and research with foggy thought, sloppy prose, and spelling or grammatical errors.

The doctoral dissertation, although some allow the originality requirement and the length of the work to overwhelm them, is basically just a specific kind of writing for which you must adhere to a unique set of guidelines. A few hours spent studying copies of dissertations by others in your discipline at your university library will teach you a great deal about the style expected by your school. Most schools distribute lists of specifications for final dissertations that must be fulfilled in order for the document to be deposited for the degree.

It's important to approach the dissertation as you would any complicated and demanding writing task. If not, short-term school and career dilemmas and long-term writing-related problems may result, such as the ones described by a college teacher who has been blocked for six years since he finally finished his dissertation: "The dissertation in some ways really created my writer's block. In graduate school and even before, I would write sixty-page papers. I used to get complaints from professors about the size of the papers. [Before the dissertation] I used to love to write."

EXERCISES

1. Analyze the following personal letter to a friend in another country. Note whether it succeeds in terms of content, clarity, appropriateness, and readability.

March 2

Dear ———,

How are you? It's been a while since I've heard from you and I don't know who's turn it is to write. Did I thank you for your lovely Season's Greetings card?
Tell me about your family's agency? the hotel? your children? Brian? What reading are you doing these days? Any plans to go to Europe or the States?
Sorry this is so short but I wanted to at least reestablish communication and say "hi."

Your friend, ———

P.S. Have you seen the film *Gandhi* yet?

How might you rewrite the above letter so it is a more effective medium of communication? What stylistic changes might enhance its readability? Are there phrases that you would rewrite because they are trite, offensive, or inappropriate?

2. Use the space below to write down at least three closings other than "Sincerely yours" or "Yours truly" that would be appropriate for business letters:

---

3. Rewrite a memo that you have distributed recently, revising it so that it is more effective writing.

4. Find a report that you recently wrote or received and edit it to reflect some of the techniques for effective report writing that you have learned in this chapter (such as including an abstract, using titles and subheads, enlivening your text with quotations, anecdotes, or illustrations).

REFERENCES

Blicq, Ron S. *Guidelines for Report Writers: A Complete Manual for On-the-Job Report Writing.* Englewood Cliffs, New Jersey: Prentice-Hall, Inc., 1982.

Cypert, Samuel A. *Writing Effective Business Letters, Memos, Proposals, & Reports.* Chicago: Contemporary Books, 1983.

Davis, Gordon B., and Clyde A. Parker. *Writing the Doctoral Dissertation.* Woodbury, New York: Barron's Educational Series, Inc., 1979.

Ewing, David W. *Writing for Results in Business, Government, and the Professions.* New York: John Wiley & Sons, Inc., 1974. An extensive reference dealing with the content and style issues of nonfiction writing in business settings.

Fruehling, Rosemary T., and Sharon Bouchard. *The Art of Writing Effective Letters.* New York: McGraw-Hill Book Company, 1972.

Mager, N.H., and S.K. Mager. *The Complete Letter Writer.* New York: Pocket Books, 1968.

Sigband, Norman B. *Communication for Management and Business.* 3rd ed. Glenview: Scott, Foresman and Company, 1982. A basic text, with supplementary readings, covering oral and written communication in a business setting, including writing and editing for results, research techniques and reports for decision making, and business, sales, and goodwill letters.

Strenski, Ellen, and Madge Manfred. *The Research Paper Workbook.* New York: Longman, Inc., 1981. An illustrated guide, with worksheets, on writing research papers, including getting started, using existing sources, collecting firsthand information, and writing a thesis statement.

Sternberg, David. *How to Complete and Survive a Doctoral Dissertation.* New York: St. Martin's Press, 1981. Many of the procedures detailed, such as choosing a topic and developing a support group of fellow writers, would be beneficial if applied to dissertations and other nonfiction writing projects.

Turabian, Kate L. *A Manual for Writers of Term Papers, Theses, and Dissertations,* 4th ed. Chicago: University of Chicago Press, 1968.

7

Getting Your Writing Published

A kindergarten teacher is delighted when her original songs and commentary appear in a teacher's magazine. A business major receives one hundred dollars from a craft magazine for her article on making stick puppets. A therapist receives a call from a potential patient who liked the ideas she expressed in an article he just read. A rabbi is so grieved by his son's premature death he synthesizes his wisdom and provides inspiration to millions. There are as many motives for publishing your writing as there are for writing in the first place. Earning extra money or becoming a full-time professional nonfiction writer are just two reasons; you may wish to publish for career advancement, the thrill of a byline, local or national recognition, or in order to share your research or ideas with others.

Right now, getting published may still seem like an unattainable dream—or perhaps, you have enough to say that you think you should have been published years ago. Perhaps both these statements are valid to a degree. You may think that editors are unapproachable; that you must have an agent, or friends in high places; or that getting published is locked up unless you are part of a literary circle. It may seem difficult to get published at all, and certainly it is even harder to become a rich or famous author, yet anyone can get their ideas or manuscripts at least to the first line, the editors. In short, editors need writers to exist. Without authors, they cannot compile magazines, develop books for publication, or provide copy to fill up certain sections of their newspapers. There are, of course, publications that are staff-written. Some publishers even have staff authors (though these tend to be reference-book publishers). Publishers of trade (or popular), text, and technical books rely upon scholars, experts, or anyone with an interesting story to tell or information to share. The good news is that nonfiction has a better chance of being published than fiction. Of the approximately forty thousand new books published in the United States in a year, about thirty-seven thousand are nonfiction. Magazines rely on nonfiction articles, mostly from nonstaff, or freelance, writers. Your first step in getting published is deciding that you really can get your toe in the door.

Now the bad news. It is increasingly difficult to get an unsolicited manuscript (a manuscript that comes in "over the transom" without an agent, into the well-known slush pile) read, let alone accepted and published. Publishers have cut back on the staff whose job it used to be to read through the slush pile for that rare find. (Scholarly journals, which rely almost completely on unsolicited submissions, take into account the overhead for reading unsolicited manuscripts by charging would-be authors a nonrefundable submission fee of from ten to twenty-five dollars.) Moreover, you will probably have to write in your spare time, for starters or forever, since few writers are able to support themselves on their earnings. A survey of writers in the late 1970s, for example, revealed that only fifteen hundred persons were able to support themselves through the sale of their articles and books; over twenty thousand authors wrote part-time in addition to pursuing another career.

Although the chances of selling your nonfiction writing are somewhat dependent on supply and demand and the overall economic picture, there are still a lot of opportunities for your nonfiction writing to be published in newspapers, Sunday supplements, magazines, journals, or books.

Back to the toe in the door, or getting an audience, question: You can try marketing your manuscripts yourself, or you can try to get a literary agent, someone who—for ten or fifteen percent of your sales—will do the legwork for you. However, you usually need to have a track record to get a good agent to invest time and energy in trying to sell your properties. Initially, you may have to find editors on your own, since agents depend on commission: Ten percent of nothing is still nothing. Later on, unless your agent handles magazine articles (and many do not), you may have an agent for your books and still do the contacting and submitting of shorter pieces on your own. If your dream materializes—if at some point you have been published enough and the response to your work has been positive—editors and agents may start approaching you with assignments and ideas. If you still want to go the agent route, you might consider going to a newer agent who is building his or her client list rather than an established one who only wants to take on name or best-selling authors. Since you and your agent are both up-and-coming, such a marriage might work out for both of you.

If you have other sources of income and your earnings from writing are extra, you may initially prefer to gain experience writing without thoughts of publishing, completing a finished manuscript or at least the first draft with few concerns about who will eventually publish it. At some point, however, you will have to consider your specific audience. Let's say you're doing research. You've written up the research for your own work, school, or business needs, and now you want to rework that research for publication. First you have to decide where to offer the material, since every publication has a different audience and often a preferred writing style. You might write to the publication in question, enclosing a self-addressed, stamped envelope, and request what is called "author's guidelines," "guidelines for submissions," or an "author's style sheet." (Make sure you study back issues of that magazine, newspaper, or journal for content and style.) You may decide to rework your manuscript on your own according to the specifications given and send in the completed piece on speculation.

Remember, whether getting a go-ahead or submitting a finished manuscript that is accepted and published, whether you get money up front or see it upon acceptance, you cannot become a professional unless you take rejection well. *You* are not being rejected, just a specific idea or piece of writing. (The reasons for rejection may not even have much to do with your writing but be due instead to other factors, like a magazine going out of business or having recently printed another story on too similar a topic.) Concentrate on what you write and how you write and see rejection as progress, not failure. If you're unwilling to risk rejections, you will be unlikely to win the much coveted acceptances. If this is true for you, I am asking you to accomplish just by reading this book the change in philosophy that I took years to muster: to regard rejection as something you need not be ashamed of. This attitude will make your professional writing more enjoyable and less traumatic. Your ego will not be on the line with each and every assignment or project. The text of this rejection letter was sent to me from a national magazine:

Thank you for letting us see your article
entitled ''Why Do People Complain?'' We
read it with interest; but, unfortunately,
the piece does not fit in with our editorial plans at this time.

I am returning the manuscript to you with
our best wishes for publication elsewhere.
Thank you for thinking of _____.
                                    Sincerely,

                    _____

                                    Managing Editor

The article in question was eventually sold, with minor revisions, to a news syndicate and was published in several newspapers throughout the United States. Of course, not all rejections become acceptances; most writers have one, several, or many unpublished pieces, and perhaps even a book or two lying around in their drawers or closets. It is the sum total of your successful efforts that will count in the long run, not the rejections. I had wanted to work out my ideas about complaining regardless of whether an editor or readers shared my ideas. Thus, in this instance, writing the piece was initially more important to me than getting it published.

You may, however, want to take a more conservative approach and write up only something in which an editor has expressed an interest. If you wish to, write ahead, synopsizing your idea and approach, and get a go-ahead before you send in the completed material. This is called sending a query letter.

THE QUERY LETTER

Submitting a query letter is one way to find out if an editor or decision maker is interested in what you are proposing to write. Even if you have already written the whole work, you may wish to write a query letter to save the time and postage required to submit the whole manuscript. A query letter involves a short statement of what you have done or propose to do, and it should include information about your background and expertise. Many editors prefer receiving a query to receiving the completed manuscript because a query takes less time to read and respond to. Make sure you answer these questions: "Why should an editor and, hence, readers care about my idea? Why should I write it?" Obviously the expertise an editor is looking for will depend on the kind of nonfiction writing you want to do. For a newspaper story, for example, just the fact that you can write and that you can go out and get the story may be enough. The journalist is relying on the expertise of others as well as on basic reporting skills; he or she need not be a criminologist to report on a murder in Chicago.

Treat the query letter seriously. This is your sales letter. Perhaps the lead paragraph to your article, or the first paragraph and the theme of your book, should begin the letter: try to grab the interest of the editor right away. Make the query letter as well written, as carefully constructed, and as well researched as your final piece. After all, if you fail to interest an editor with your query letter, he or she will be reluctant to believe that you can excite them with the finished manuscript.

Another question you may have is, "To whom do I send the query letter?" Let's say you want to write a magazine article. The best way to make sure you're sending it to the right person is to call the magazine and inquire directly and specifically. You should also look through past issues to see (a) if your idea has been done recently and (b) if this particular magazine is the right market for your idea. Right in your query letter, show that you are familiar with the market to which you are submitting. If you are sending a query about a book proposal, and you saw the editor's name acknowledged in a similar book, or a book on a related theme, state that right in your query. In short, answer this question in the editor's mind: "Why is this writer sending this to *me?*"

Consider sending a cover letter along with a second page that is actually the query. This approach minimizes retyping, since you have to write and type only a new cover letter for another market if the query is rejected by the first person you send it to and you want to send it to someone else. Word processors, since they facilitate reworking and retyping, minimize the need for this two-page approach; many editors say they prefer just a page, especially for magazine or newspaper pieces. For a book, however, as you will see later, a lot more than a query is necessary; a formal book proposal will have to follow or be sent in place of a query letter.

I sent this query to a national magazine:

Dear Sir:

I will be in Bayreuth, Germany, in February 1972, interviewing Frau Winifred Wagner, Richard Wagner's daughter-in-law. When she was eighteen, she married Wagner's fifty-four-year-old son, Siegfried. They soon had four children. Frau Wagner is now seventy-five years old. She was a close friend of Cosima Wagner's [Richard Wagner's wife] until Cosima's death in 1933.

Frau Wagner has told me the definitive word on Richard Wagner's vegetarianism—he believed in a vegetarian diet as the saving of mankind, but his health prevented him from pursuing a meatless diet. She will be able to give details of Wagner's personal life.

What has life been like for the daughter-in-law of Richard Wagner, who lives on a fortune of twelve and a half million marks? Who are some of the famous people she has met and loved? Who are some of the famous opera singers she has known through the years as the grande dame of Wagnerian opera? What is her favorite Wagner opera?

Would your magazine be interested in an article based on my interview with Frau Wagner?

Sincerely yours,

My query received the following response from the editor:

I can't commission a Winifred Wagner interview sight unseen from a writer I haven't read, but let me say that since she so rarely grants interviews I'd very much like to see whatever you succeed in bringing back.

That article, my first nonfiction magazine credit, was researched and written on speculation, that is, without any financial commitment from a publisher: at my own risk.

There are, of course, ways to present your ideas other than through the query letter. If you have an idea that is really topical, you might, for example, telephone an editor to find out if there is any interest. Even if interest is expressed, you may still be asked to submit a written query to follow up the phone conversation. You do, however, have an indication of an editor's interest as well as the advantage of the suggestions or feedback you gleaned from your phone conversation. Editors are extremely busy, so use this telephone approach with great caution. If your idea is truly right for the market, or if you have a scoop that an editor will appreciate being offered, the telephone can be an effective tool, though it is doubtful that the beginning writer will be told to go ahead before putting it in writing. If you abuse the telephone, however, you risk being labeled a nuisance and someone to be avoided.

Another way of approaching editors is to attend lectures, conferences, and courses geared to getting published or to writing nonfiction. Editors often teach these courses or appear as guest lecturers, and one of their motives is to cultivate new or previously unpublished talent. It is still possible that an editor whom you've approached after his or her lecture or speech will tell you to send a query. Even if you don't get further than this, at least you have made some personal contact, and you can remind the editor of your initial meeting as a point of departure for your query. Editors will usually only ask you to follow up an idea that you have stated verbally with a written query if they *do* have interest. Every written query necessitates a rejection or acceptance, work for the editor and his or her assistants or secretaries, and there is a reluctance among editors to generate unnecessary paperwork.

As a starry-eyed and unpublished young writer, I attended the very first nonfiction writers workshop sponsored by the American Society of Journalists and Authors (ASJA) in December 1971. It was a thrill to listen to the expert advice of published authors as well as to encounter real live buying editors.

Betty Frank, who was then an editor at *Good Housekeeping,* explained how articles are conceived and commissioned, and why they are rejected, at her magazine. I went up to her after her talk and told her about an idea I had for an article. She expressed interest in seeing it on speculation, and I tripped over myself with euphoria that a real live editor was interested in what I had to say. Although she promptly rejected the article—as did several other magazines in the next year or two—it eventually became the theme of my book on crime victims, which was finally published in 1978.

MARKETS

Newspapers and Sunday Supplements

Although most newspapers are staff-written, there are often pages or sections of each paper that are not only open to but depend on submissions by freelance (nonstaff) writers. These sections are either the editorial or viewpoint pages of a newspaper or the Sunday supplement magazine. There are also newspaper syndicates that depend on freelance nonfiction writers. Payment for these five hundred- to seven hundred-word columns (or longer, magazine-length pieces for the Sunday supplements) is usually at the lower end of the scale compared to specialized or national "slick" magazines like *Family Circle, Redbook, Playboy, Working Woman,* or *Better Homes and Gardens.* However, because of the daily demands of filling the paper, newspapers offer one of the most viable markets for new writers. Although you may get only a hundred dollars for a short article or first-person essay that may have taken weeks to research, you will have a clip (an example of your published work) to send around next time you submit a query or a finished manuscript for consideration. Clips carry weight with editors. Second, if you are aiming to get published in your local newspaper, you will have the added advantage of being able to write stories or conduct interviews with persons who either read the publication or have a local slant, so that readers will relate more easily to your research and be more affected by the issues that you might explore (such as pollution by a local plant or where to go on weekends within an hour's drive from the community).

Local newspaper reporters are rarely given the time to explore stories or issues in the depth that freelancers can, especially if the freelancer is more concerned with the final story than with how much time, energy, or money will go into digging for it. Similarly, specialized "trade" weekly newspapers are markets you should consider, since the need for in-depth copy is acute for these publications as well. Although the pay may be low or nonexistent, you will have readers interested in your field, and possibly new assignments generated by other editors who see your piece and contact you because of it.

Consider writing a letter to the editor of your local newspaper. Letters to the editor have sometimes resulted in assignments for longer works (or even books) developed from the theme that the writer expressed. Incidentally, until you have those clips from *The New York Times* or *McCall's* to show, a published letter to the editor (if that is your only credit) is at least a published example of your writing. As you probably know, you do *not* send a query letter regarding a letter to the editor. Many newspapers also instruct you that only letters that are accepted will be acknowledged; the others may not even be returned. You can increase the likelihood that your letter to the editor is accepted if you write it as if it is the most important writing assignment you have been given, applying to it the same concern for content and style that you would apply to a magazine article or book. Include your name, address, and phone number, since most newspapers do telephone checks to assure the identity of a letter's author.

Here are general guidelines for trying to get published in newspapers or slick magazines. These suggestions apply to specialized markets as well:

- *Study the magazine.* Know your market (your audience). Read current and back issues. Take notes on the kinds of articles that appear, being especially careful that you do not suggest an article on a topic that has been covered in recent issues. If your topic *does* cover familiar territory, make sure you have a fresh, controversial, and grabbing angle.

- *Decide to whom you should submit your idea.* Read the masthead, or call, to find out which specific editor (e.g., food, articles, exercise, health and beauty) you should submit to.
- *Write a query letter or contact an editor.* It's more efficient to get some feedback on your idea before you pursue it further. Even if you have written a first draft of your article, you may wish to rewrite it after learning of a magazine's particular interests.
- *Enclose published clips.* If you have published anything before that you think reflects well on your writing abilities, send along a sample. If you lack any published samples, or if your published work is not representative of your improved writing style, include the first two or three paragraphs of your article. Remember that the query letter sells the idea; published writing samples or the first few paragraphs of your proposed article demonstrate that you will be able to carry out the assignment.
- *Be professional about rejections or assignments.* Don't besiege the editor with questions about why your query was rejected, although some are nice enough to state the reasons quite explicitly, while others only send a perfunctory or form letter. If you do get a go-ahead, discuss fee, deadline, format, length, etc., just as you would discuss any assignment from a teacher or employer. (Magazines have technical considerations, especially length and deadlines, that you will have to adhere to.)
- *Submit neat, clean copy on or before your deadline.* Although an acceptance is not guaranteed just because your manuscript is neatly typed and is in on time, at least you will give your work the best chance possible. The effort is worthwhile: A successful assignment may lead to others with the same editor and publication.
- *If accepted, try to land another assignment while your good track record is fresh in the editor's mind.*
- *Resist inclinations to become arrogant, or to become a full-time professional writer, because of one sale.* There are certainly those who *do* quit their jobs and go on to successful freelance writing careers after just one sale, but the risk factor is likely to be too high for you. Generally, one article (or even one book) does not a career make, so be

conservative about what one sale means in your long-range career/writing plans. You should also remember that you may have to follow these same guidelines whether you are trying to sell your second or your seventieth article. The excitement, and the woe, of writing are that you always have to prove yourself again.

"Slick" Magazines

The "slick," or mass-market, magazines are the ones with the largest budgets for writers, the biggest circulation, and the greatest competition for a byline. All the rules for approaching editors, writing queries, and submitting the best manuscript possible in terms of content and style apply here, and then some. The "then some" comes in because the budget for these magazines is so much larger than that for smaller-scale operations that they are able to commission more articles than they can possibly use (for some magazines the excess is as high as fifty percent). The mass-market magazines also accept and buy articles to put in inventory. This means the articles will be on hand for use if some other article falls through. So even accepted articles may never be published. (If you have an agent, or if you are a good negotiator, you can usually request the release of your article if it has not been published within a year after acceptance, even if you have been paid in full.)

Unless you come to a slick through an agent or have a good track record, you will probably have to send a query letter to get a go-ahead to write on speculation, which means that you will have to write the entire article with little hope that you will earn anything for your efforts. More seasoned writers can sometimes get a "kill fee" clause in their agreement: If the article assigned does not get accepted for any reason, the writer will be paid part of an agreed-upon fee (usually 25 percent, sometimes as high as 50 percent). Getting that first assignment for a slick can be as fortuitous as getting your first nonfiction book contract. It can also be as mundane as sending a query, getting a go-ahead, and having the finished piece accepted and subsequently published. My first assignment for a slick evolved out of looking for a job as an editor. Part of the application procedure for an editorial position on *McCall's* "Right Now" section was to think up possible stories for that section. I, of course, studied current and back issues and submitted thirteen possible ideas to them. I did not get the editing job, but I was asked to write up my thirteenth idea and to submit it as a freelance assignment. (That idea was suggested by my mother. She had seen a little filler in a newspaper column relating what had been said about Neil Simon in his high school yearbook and wondered what had been said in high school yearbooks about others who had gone on to become celebrated in various fields.) This idea became my first published nonfiction article in a slick magazine, and I was paid two hundred dollars for it.

Specialized Magazines

Specialized magazines give you the advantage of knowing in advance for whom you are writing. These magazines may not have the glamour or the high pay scale that you will find with the slicks, but sales are often easier if you choose an appropriate idea to write about. (That, as you may recall, was why I was successful in placing my interview with Richard Wagner's daughter-in-law in an opera magazine.) Guidelines for query letters or rules for submission of completed manuscripts may be specified by the market (the particular magazine), or you might just have to follow solid advice for submitting to any magazine. You should, of course, be familiar with current and past issues of the magazine you submit to. You should have access to any of the annual directories of specialized magazines that include basic information about exact name, address, editors' names and, in more detailed directories, kinds of material that they can use, guidelines for submission, range of pay, etc. Such directories include: *Writer's Market* (updated annually) (Cincinnati, Ohio: Writer's Digest Books); *The International Directory of Little Magazines and Small Presses* (updated periodically) (Paradise, Calif.: Dustbooks); and *LMP/Literary Market Place* (updated annually) (New York: R.R. Bowker Company).

Journals

Recognize at once that payment for publication in a journal is usually very low and often only in copies of the journal instead of in cash. As noted before, for some monthly or quarterly journals, you may even have to pay a nonrefundable fee of from ten dollars to twenty-five dollars for having your manuscript considered. Those who want to, or need to, publish in professional journals are probably well enough aware of the career benefits of this kind of publishing that I need not discuss them here. Journals practice the know-your-audience maxim: They (and you) know exactly who will read your proposed writing. Publishing in specialized journals need not rule out publishing for other markets, especially more popular ones. It does, however, offer benefits that publishing for monetary gain may not afford you, that is, getting your research activities and opinions across to your peers, and prestige. I suggest you view the fact that each journal has a definite audience as an advantage to your writing efforts.

Some would-be authors, however, are discouraged by the fact that journals, unlike a lot of other publications, are usually clear and explicit about the submission procedures for their publication. (It can, indeed, be frustrating that an article rejected by one journal must be virtually retyped or rewritten just to conform to the strict stylistic demands—footnotes, listing of references, placement of charts, etc.—of another if you decide to submit elsewhere.) Take those guidelines seriously, but regard them as structural impositions. Certain rules must be observed whatever kind of nonfiction writing you do: You need "front matter" or an index for a book-length manuscript, heading and salutation for a business letter, and so on. You will usually find journal guidelines spelled out in a recent issue of the publication (most publish their guidelines at least once a year), or you can write to the editor and request a list of guidelines (manuscript specifications).

If you do not have the time or inclination to write an entire article on speculation for a professional journal, or if you are not currently engaged in research that would warrant such a full-length work, consider doing book reviews for specific journals. Each journal has a book review editor and a specific policy about how books are assigned for review. (For some journals, for example, you can write to the book review editor asking to review a specific title. In this query letter, as in all others, you would explain why the book should be reviewed and what credentials you have for being the person to do it.) Other journals keep a roster of reviewers and assign specific titles to the reviewer of their choice. Since book review editors do change, you should consider writing a letter to the journals you are interested in to find out how you go about getting on their list of reviewers. A one-page résumé and a copy of any published writings that seem appropriate should be included. If your review is published, your only payment may be the price of the book you are asked to review, which you are usually sent free and allowed to keep. However, you will have a publication credit and your writing style and analytical abilities and expertise will have been exposed to your peers.

Most professional societies publish a list of journals related to their members' interests, including the name, address, and telephone number of the journal, its current editor, and any established submission policies writers should be aware of. Contact your professional association to find out if such a list exists.

Multiple submissions of query letters or completed manuscripts to journals is rarely allowed. Slick magazines and book publishers consider multiple submission a gray area: some discourage it, but others don't. Unfortunately, unless you want to risk incurring the wrath of your colleagues, a "one-at-a-time" policy of submission (and resubmission to another market only upon rejection and return of your query or manuscript) should be observed.

FORMAT FOR SUBMISSIONS

The following general guidelines for preparing manuscripts apply to newspapers, specialized or slick magazines, and book publishers. (Journals, as already noted, will often spell out their specific format guidelines.) If you have access to a word processor, some of the steps spelled out below can be avoided or facilitated (if you have software that corrects spelling, for example).

1. Make your written submissions look professional, whether or not you have been published before. The appearance *and* the content/style of everything you give an editor should be of professional quality.
2. Type everything. (If you have a word processor, letter quality print is preferable to dot matrix.)
3. Double-space all submissions (except query letters, which are, like most business letters, single-spaced).
4. Use white heavyweight paper (twenty-pound bond), not corrasable or erasable paper (it smudges and is harder to read).

5. Use a black, fresh ribbon.
6. Keep wide margins (two inches from the top; one inch from the sides and bottom).
7. Make sure your name is on the front page of the manuscript. Your last name should be at the top corner of each page, before the page number (which must be given in standard numerical sequence).
8. Even if you do enclose a cover letter with your name, address, and phone number, make sure this information appears somewhere on your manuscript in case the editor has to contact you.
9. Submit your original to the editor. Keep a carbon or photocopy for your files.
10. All submissions should be letter-perfect. All spelling and grammatical errors should be corrected and your manuscript retyped if necessary before it is submitted. As with any nonfiction writing, these are the stages in manuscript preparation:

    Writing
    Editing
    Rewriting
    Retyping
    Final proofreading
    Final typing

11. If possible, include at the time of manuscript submission any signed permission forms or accompanying photographs or illustrations.
12. Except for actual assignments, all submissions to editors must be accompanied by a self-addressed, stamped envelope with the proper postage. It's usually best to mail submissions flat rather than in a legal-size envelope, even those of just one or two pages. For assignments, enclose a self-addressed, stamped postcard, to be returned to you indicating that your material arrived.

BOOK PUBLISHERS

Excluding the author's advance, if there is one, a publisher's financial investment in physically producing a nonfiction book of average length—straight text, no fancy photos or illustrations—

may be anywhere from ten thousand to twenty thousand dollars today. This estimate excludes any advertising, publicity, or promotion for the book (which could be double or triple the cost of production), and the salaries of the staff or freelance editors necessary to bring the book from idea through to publication. Is it any wonder that publishers need to be sure, especially with unknown writers, that there will be some return on their investment?

The first book you sell may not net a big advance for your efforts, which sometimes include years and years of research and the acquiring of expertise, because there may be insufficient confidence that you will be able to complete a book-length manuscript, and you do not yet have a sales or track record to bargain with. (If you have self-discipline and a strong belief in your idea, it might be financially better in the long run to complete the book and then try to sell it. At least you won't have to worry about whether you can, in fact, follow through on a book-length assignment.) Even if you have a track record, the competition in the nonfiction book area is fierce, and publishers want as much assurance as possible not only that you will finish the manuscript, but that it will be thoroughly researched and worthy of the time, effort, and money spent publishing it. Although an experienced author may be able to sell a book on the basis of a one-page outline and synopsis, beginning nonfiction writers (and, in these economically insecure times, even some accomplished ones) will have to expect to write a detailed table of contents, a synopsis, and a chapter or two.

Before discussing the outline and synopsis, I want to answer the question most commonly asked by would-be book authors: "How do I find a publisher?" A first step might be to consult *LMP, Literary Market Place,* a comprehensive guide to the American book industry published annually by R. R. Bowker. *LMP* lists American book publishers and briefly indicates their specialties. It also contains a directory of literary agents. As we've seen, it is very difficult—though not impossible—to place a manuscript yourself without a "track record"; on the other hand, persuading a good agency to handle your work can also be a struggle. Whichever route you choose, you will need persistence.

Dr. Hank Greene, a former physical-education administrator who up to then had published only a few short articles in specialized newspapers and magazines, is one of the few people I know of who actually sold his book "over the transom." Hank, who has his doctorate from Columbia University as well as years of professional experience in the square-dance field, wrote such an effective query letter, outline, and sample chapter for Harper & Row that they responded immediately. A contract was signed and he got an excellent advance for a new book author. Hank beat the odds.

The story behind my first published nonfiction book is somewhat different. My book grew out of a speech that I gave in my junior year of college. My speech teacher gave the same advice about writing a speech as I, and most other writing teachers, have given you about nonfiction writing: Speak about what you are interested in, what you know. I was interested in vegetarianism and since I didn't know very much about it, I went to the library to see what research had been done. I was fascinated to learn that there had been treatises written on vegetarianism by such esteemed and diverse vegetarians as Percy Bysshe Shelley, George Bernard Shaw, Mahatma Gandhi, and Richard Wagner. The speech was a success, and I continued researching the history of vegetarianism in my spare time over the next few years, traveling around the world to conduct interviews, canvassing obscure and comprehensive libraries whenever I happened to be in another city. I knew I wanted to publish a book about the subject, and at the time that I began teaching a course in the history of vegetarianism at the New School in New York, I was discouraged about ever finding a publisher. I had decided to teach the course because I wanted to make some use of the four drawers of research material that I had accumulated in my filing cabinet. The announcement of my course was, as is the usual policy, published in the school bulletin for fall 1973. Before I even set foot in the classroom for the first time, a letter arrived from a book editor proposing that we meet to discuss the prospect of a book.

I spoke with the editor, who explained to me that she wanted an outline of my book, as well as a completed chapter or two. Because I had been researching the topic for so many years—I had even worked on a few chapters—I was able to sit down and, in a few very long sittings, write a hundred-page outline of my proposed book. Within a short time I was offered a contract. The editor and I met, and she brought along the first part of my advance with the contract, an event I have since learned is rare in publishing. One thousand dollars may not seem like a lot of money to get excited about after years of research. (Fortunately, the book did earn royalties after it was published here and in British and Dutch editions.) It was, however, a chance to break into print and to complete a project that had been a driving force in my life for many years.

A query letter to see if a publisher is interested in the topic you are writing about, followed by a chapter-by-chapter outline of your proposed book (and, if necessary, a sample completed chapter), may seem like a lot for a publisher to ask without having paid any money or even having given a commitment to publish. This system will, however, get your idea a hearing, and it may even justify a larger advance from the publisher's point of view: If an editor has a very strong positive response to your material, the publisher may offer a generous advance in order to secure the book.

The best way to understand what a book proposal should look like is to see an example of one. The proposal I've chosen as an example is the one I wrote for my fifth book, *Single in America*, which was published by Atheneum in 1980. The first two pages of the proposal (not included here) detailed my past writing credits as well as information about my professional and personal background that I thought would "sell" me to the publisher as an author. This proposal (somewhat edited for length considerations) follows the guidelines for writing book proposals in that it tells the editor exactly what I wanted to write about in the book, chapter by chapter; it contains examples of the kinds of anecdotes, quotations, and research material that I planned to cover; it explains why I thought the book should be written, who its readers (audience/market) would be, and how I planned to collect my facts (data).

SINGLE IN AMERICA by J.L. Barkas

Table of Contents

Preface   Why Am I Single?
Introduction   The Single Epidemic
Transitional Singleness
1   Postponed Marriage
2   Separated
Situational Singleness
3   Divorced
4   Widowed
5   Never Married
---
6   Singleness Within All Re-
               lationships
7   The Effects of Singleness
Conclusion   Predictions for the Future
Bibliography
Index

SINGLE IN AMERICA: SYNOPSIS

Between 1970 and 1976, the number of men and women living alone in the United States increased by forty percent. Single adults now total about twenty-one percent of all households, or about fifty million persons. SINGLE IN AMERICA will offer an objective, comprehensive, and penetrating analysis of this growing trend toward singleness. Its conclusions will be drawn from hundreds of interviews around the country with single men and women of all kinds and ages--college students; singles in their twenties, thirties, forties, and older; divorcees; widows and widowers; those who are separated or divorced; and so forth. Those interviewees will be contrasted with men and women who are living together but unmarried, as well as with married couples and same-sex

partners. Background research and
interviews with experts--sociologists,
psychologists, psychiatrists, and physi-
cians--will provide perspective in my
examinations of the problems and positive
experiences of single people.

SINGLE IN AMERICA is not a book about
loneliness, such as Gordon's Lonely in
America. Nor will its format resemble The
Hite Report. It will include men and
women, since singleness is not a state re-
served for women.

There is certainly interest in the
growth of singleness. Clichés about loneliness and the ''free single life''
abound. Samuel Kaplan in The Washington
Post even noted his fear that ''It is now
apparently time for singles to be ex-
ploited.'' But a thorough and serious
study of the psychological and social effects of singleness on the individual, the
family, and our entire culture is not yet
available. Its necessity is highlighted in
Joanna Kyd's concluding words in her New
York Times essay, ''Unmarriage'': ''Marriages don't seem to work anymore, but
there's a new lost generation that grows
bigger every day. Because the truth is
that unmarriage doesn't work either.''

With the insights gained from my interviews, I will take singleness one step
further and develop a typology of motivations for singleness. Statistics confirm
that we have come out of the ''emancipa-
tion period''--marriage is no longer
''necessary.'' SINGLE IN AMERICA will demonstrate whether the single alternative is
better or worse than traditional marriage
and, perhaps, suggest a third and new alternative.

SINGLE IN AMERICA: OUTLINE

PREFACE: Why Am I Single?

The preface will be an honest self-analysis of my single years. The style will resemble that of the preface of Victims. I am willing to share some of both my horrific and my exhilarating experiences as a single woman. This will start the book with a self-interview. The intention will be to offset the half-truths about singleness that are so frequently espoused today. Some of the issues I will deal with include coping with celibacy as well as ''sexual liberation''; financial independence; social and professional harassments and predicaments because of being single; misuse or overuse of girlfriends during the periods between boyfriends; and coming to grips with what being single means to me.

INTRODUCTION: The Single Epidemic

In New York City alone, there are over 700,000 single men and women. Some 17 percent of all children--one in six--are living in single-parent families. It is also predicted that 45 percent of those children born in 1977 will live in a single-parent family sometime before the age of eighteen. By 1976, there was one divorce for every two marriages in the United States. There are also an estimated ten to twenty million homosexuals, 1.8 million widowers, five times as many widows; and the number of couples living together, but unmarried, increased from 523,000 in 1970 to 957,000 in 1977. Those

are just some of the statistics that will
be cited and discussed in this introductory chapter on the ''epidemic'' of singleness. Contrasts with other countries,
such as England and West Germany, will
show whether singleness is an American or
multinational development.

TRANSITIONAL SINGLENESS

CHAPTER 1: Postponed Marriage
    First-marriage rates have continued to
decline and, since 1960, the number of
women still single at ages twenty to
twenty-four has increased by 50 percent.
Through interviews with high school and
college students, I plan to reveal their
attitudes on marriage. Where does marriage
fit into the future plans of America's
youth? How do they view singleness? Those
perspectives will be contrasted with
surveys and studies of students conducted
in the forties, fifties, and sixties.
Since the adult population of tomorrow
will be composed of these youngsters, some
insights into the temporary or permanent
expansion of singleness will be
substantiated.

CHAPTER 2: Separated
    There are two major themes to this
chapter: the experiences of the separated
person who may or may not return to his or
her marriage, and separation within every
person's life, whether married or single.
It will also be interesting to interview
men and women who prefer separation to
divorce and to reveal the psychological
and economic motivations behind

maintaining separation as a permanent, not
a transitional, situation.

SITUATIONAL SINGLENESS

CHAPTER 3: Divorced
  From 1962 to 1976, there was a 127
percent increase in the divorce rate in
the United States. Yet four out of every
five divorced persons remarry. On the
other hand, redivorce is higher among
second marriages, and the chance of
remarriage drops for women after age
thirty and after thirty-five for men. So
there are two contrasting situations here:
divorce as a transitional single state
between marriages and divorce as the
beginning of permanent singleness. Through
interviews, I will probe how recently and
longtime divorced persons (with and
without children) view their singleness.
Those interviews, and their reflections on
their marriages, will be contrasted with
interviews with married couples.

CHAPTER 4: Widowed
  The nearly two million widowers in the
United States have 174,000 of their own
children under eighteen years old living
with them. Although the elderly come to
mind when widowhood is mentioned,
accidents and crime have increased the
number of women widowed before age forty.
Interviews with widows and widowers will
cover all age groups and the four major
causes of death: accident, ''natural''
causes (health-related), homicide, and
suicide. Women outnumber men in this
category of singleness by five to one, but
the death rate of widowers above the age

of forty-five is double that of married
men. Do the widowed long for a second
union in the same way as the divorced or
the never-married might wish for a spouse?
Does the circumstance that provoked sin-
gleness--death--decrease or increase the
problems associated with singleness? Are
the elderly living together without marriage as numerous as has been rumored?

CHAPTER 5: Never Married
  ''I'm free as a bird,'' says one
thirty-five-year-old never-married woman.
''I am not answerable to anyone. But I'm
not free. Because of a lack of intimacy, I
am not fulfilled in that area and that
curtails my freedom. Being single means
you have to find meaning in activities,
rather than in growing with somebody
else.'' This chapter will be based on
interviews with those who have never
married, and those who never plan to
marry--nuns, priests, and homosexuals.
Their opinions and descriptions will be
used as a contrast to other groups of
singles and marrieds. How do
never-marrieds compare with those who see
singleness as a temporary condition?

CHAPTER 6: Singleness Within
All Relationships
  This is not a ''how-to'' chapter but an
exploration of the concept of
individuality and singleness and how it
relates to all single or plural
relationships. It is my belief that a
distortion of single = independent and
marriage = dependent may be one factor in
the proliferation--and current
illusions--of singleness. If

individuality (singleness) means ''not related to other people,'' what does this
imply? How do you develop independence?
preserve it? reintroduce it into your single or married situation?

CHAPTER 7: The Effect of
Singleness
   The conclusions in this chapter will be
drawn from the interviews and data
presented in the previous parts of this
book. From that information, I will be
able to answer how singleness affects the
individual, the family, and society. For
example, is it true that single men and
women have more psychosomatic ailments
than married persons? Do single people die
sooner? Is loneliness a universal
consequence of singleness? Does singleness
affect work? other relationships?
child-rearing practices? How does lack of
intimacy in a heterosexual relationship
affect self-image? How do the children of
single-parent families compare with the
children in more traditional two-parent
households? What about children raised by
single mothers versus single fathers? How
has the increase in the number of single
adult households affected the nation's
economy? media? migration trends? crime
rate? eating habits?

CONCLUSION: Predictions for
the Future
   I am unable now to cite what these
conclusions will be, but I will predict
whether singleness will grow or decrease
in the future and discuss the positive or
negative effects of that development. I
will also determine as a result of

researching and writing this book whether
singleness is to be welcomed or avoided.
Whatever my conclusions, however, the
growth of singleness and its dramatic individual, family, and cultural impact demand to be objectively understood.

BIBLIOGRAPHY
   I consider this optional; if there is
one, the format it should take is open to
discussion. It could be just a listing of
major consulted works or a more in-depth,
annotated work.

Once you sign the contract, you will have to finish writing
the book. Although you will have a final deadline for submission
of your manuscript, it will be up to you to set deadlines for each
step/chapter of your manuscript along the way to that deadline.
This is where most book authors get into trouble. In order to have
a book ready in, say, one year, you will have to complete hundreds of little steps. At the point of committing yourself to the
completion of a book-length project, writing becomes as much a
time-management issue as a creative one. If you find writer's
block occurring, refer back to the discussion and solutions in
Chapter 2.
   The general schedule that follows indicates the kinds of divisions you should be making.

GENERAL BOOK-WRITING SCHEDULE

Divide the number of chapters by the amount of time you
have till your deadline.
   Take these tasks into consideration in making your schedule:

Research
   Interviews and/or observations
   Examination of existing sources

First draft
Revisions
Fact checking
Permission clearances
Final draft
Submission to outside readers for critiques
Rewriting
Submission to publisher
Minor or major revisions

As the above list indicates, once you submit your finished manuscript, you will have to wait to find out if it is acceptable. It may be accepted as is, or you may have to do some additional rewriting, researching, revising. You do, of course, have the right to disagree with any or all of the changes that your publisher (or the publisher's outside readers) suggests on your manuscript. Be careful, however, that you do not instantly reject their suggestions because of the "I've got to write it right the first time" theory. Writing is usually rewriting, even rewriting parts or chapters of a book.

After any and all finishing touches are made on the manuscript, and all necessary permission clearances have been obtained, your book will go into production. The publisher will prepare a schedule for your book, including when galleys and page proofs of your manuscript will be ready, when the typeset manuscript goes to the printer, when the printer's "blues" should be received and returned, dates for bound copies, and the date, usually six weeks later, for the published books. (That six-week period allows time to get the books into the distributors and to the stores.) The whole process, from accepted manuscript to publication, generally takes from nine months to a year. It might, of course, be made shorter because a book is particularly topical, or because the author can submit the book on floppy disks and the publisher is able to set the type directly from the computer-generated disks. The schedule might, however, be longer because of an unforeseen paper shortage, a competing title on a list, a backup at the compositor's or the printer's, and so on. (Many book contracts spell out that the book *must* be published within eighteen months of acceptance or the rights revert to the author.)

The list that follows provides a more detailed guide to the schedules and procedures required to bring your completed manuscript to a bound book. Not all of these procedures apply to every book, however. You can use this list to keep track of what is obviously a very complicated process, for your first or your fifth book project.

```
        WRITING/PUBLISHING SCHEDULE FOR A
                       BOOK

PROJECT (WORKING
TITLE):                      _____
CONTRACT SIGNED ON:          _____
MANUSCRIPT DUE DATE:         _____
FIRST DRAFT
COMPLETED ON:                _____
CRITIQUES SENT:              _____
ALL CRITIQUES IN BY:         _____
ALL PERMISSIONS
CLEARED:                     _____
PHOTOGRAPHS/ILLUSTRATIONS
IN BY:                       _____
SECOND DRAFT
COMPLETED ON:                _____
FINAL DRAFT FINISHED
ON:                          _____
MS. TO PUBLISHER ON:         _____
MS. BACK FROM EDITOR
ON:                          _____
REVIEWED MS. TO
PUBLISHER ON:                _____
PROOFS RECEIVED ON:          _____
PROOFS BACK TO
PUBLISHER ON:                _____
PUBLICITY DEPT. INFO SHEETS
(DUE 6-9 MONTHS BEFORE PUBLICATION)
SUBMITTED ON:                _____
INDEX DUE BY:                _____
BOUND BOOK DATE:             _____
PUBLICATION DATE:            _____
```

The schedule that follows is the actual schedule for my book, *Single in America*. The schedule traces the evolution of this book project from my initial meeting with the editor in April 1978, follow-up discussions with a friend that led to conceptualizing the topic, through publication of the Japanese edition of the book in December 1981.

SCHEDULE FOR <u>SINGLE IN AMERICA</u>

April 1978	Met editor at E&D's surprise party
June 2	Discussed idea during kaffeeklatsches with Jean
June 18	Proposal to Atheneum
Nov. 7	Contract signed
Dec. 28	Received 1st part of advance
April 23, 1979	Chapters 1 & 2 to editor
May 10	Lunch with editor to discuss 1 & 2
May 22	Revised Ch. 1 to editor
May 24	Received 2nd part of advance
July 21	Chapters 2-5 to editor
July 26	Chapters 1, 6-8, & Bibliography to editor
August 10	Publicity information sheet to publicist. Ms. returned with comments from editor
Sept. 10	Revised ms. submitted to editor
Sept. 10-Oct. 1	Permissions cleared
Sept. 11	Names to publicist for possible jacket blurbs
Sept. 18	Meeting with editor
Sept. 20	Additional material submitted

Sept. 21	Editor submitted cata-logue copy
Sept. 26-Nov. 18	Revising last draft of manuscript
Nov. 19	Final manuscript to edi-tor
Dec. 19	Received last part of advance
Jan. 8, 1980	Ms. received from copy editor
Jan. 18	Ms. returned to editor Add'l lists to publicity and college depts.
Jan. 21	Photocopies sent out for first serial rights
March 13	Galleys received
March 25	Jacket copy, sample jacket received
March 27	Galleys returned to edi-tor Bound galleys rec'd for serialization distribu-tion
April	Page proofs received
June	Bound book date
July 6	Syndicated 6-part series appears in newspapers
July 14, 1980	Publication date
August 6	Publication party, 5-7 PM
August 24-7	Author tour to Cleve-land, Detroit, Chicago
Dec. 1981	Japanese edition is pub-lished

The following sheet will help you to keep track of the persons with whom the fate of your book manuscript rests while it is at the publisher, and after it is sent to the bookstores:

BOOK PRODUCTION/PUBLICATION
NAME/PHONE DIRECTORY AND INFO
SHEET

TITLE: _____
PUBLISHER: _____
                           _____
                           _____

PUBLICATION DATE: _____
  Galleys: _____
  Pages: _____
  Bound book: _____
BOOK'S EDITOR: _____
  Editor's Asst.:   _____
  Editor-in-Chief: _____

AGENT: _____

PRODUCTION MANAGER: _____
  Production Editor: _____

PUBLICITY DIRECTOR: _____
  Director's Asst.:   _____
PUBLICIST ON THIS
BOOK: _____

COVER WILL BE HANDLED BY _____ DEPT.

MARKETING MANAGER: _____
SALES MANAGER: _____
ADVERTISING MGR: _____
SPECIAL SALES: _____

SUBSIDIARY RIGHTS: _____
FOREIGN RIGHTS: _____

`Additional Names/#s:` _____

_____

_____

_____

_____

`First printing:` _____

Once your book is ready for distribution, you will have to decide how much time and effort you can afford to put into the postwriting and pre- and postpublication phases of the publication of your book. As most seasoned writers know, marketing your book may be as important as writing it. Many writers see themselves as researchers and writers, not as talk-show guests or lecturers, so they prefer not to take time from writing a new work or other obligations to plug their latest book. Others simply do not have the time in their schedule to fulfill such promotional plans. Base your decision about whether to promote your writing on considered judgment, however, not on "selling block" (as one of my writing survey respondents termed the postpublication counterpart of "writer's block").

EXERCISES

1. Pick one idea for a nonfiction article or book and decide on your audience and how you would go about researching/writing something that would be worth reading. Ask yourself the question: "Why would a reader turn each page?" Decide on a market for your project and write a query letter.

2. Take a nonfiction article or book that you think is especially well researched and written. Write a query letter for that project. Outline the book and consider how you could apply these techniques to your own work.

3. Begin a file for any submissions that you make, including the rejection or acceptance letters that you receive. Some-

day you may find you too want to write something about writing. These letters will be invaluable original research with which you can back up your points, as well as a chronological guide to the evolution of your professional career. In this way, the letters editors write to you, as well as notes made during your meetings, become an individualized course in your on-the-job training as a writer.

REFERENCES

Appelbaum, Judith, and Nancy Evans. *How to Get Happily Published.* New York: Harper & Row, 1978.

Balkin, Richard. *A Writer's Guide to Book Publishing.* New York: Hawthorn Books, 1977.

Barkas, J.L. "How to Behave on Television." *Writer's Digest,* September 1975, pp. 11–13. Fourteen tips for media-shy authors to turn their talk-show experiences into "a professionally rewarding as well as a stimulating event."

Boyd, Malcolm. "How to Make a Creative Book Promotion Tour." *Publishers Weekly,* July 29, 1974, pp. 26–7. Boyd, a talk-show circuit veteran, provides advice on making the most of TV and radio book promotion tours.

Daigh, Ralph. *Maybe You Should Write a Book.* Englewood Cliffs, New Jersey: Prentice-Hall, Inc., 1977.

Dickson, Frank A. *1001 Article Ideas.* Cincinnati: Writer's Digest Books, 1979.

Gearing, Philip J., and Evelyn V. Brunson. *Breaking Into Print.* Englewood Cliffs, New Jersey: Prentice-Hall, Inc., 1977.

James, Caryn. "Publishers' Confessions—Rejections I Regret." *New York Times Book Review,* May 6, 1984, pp. 1, 34–7. Even the great book editor Maxwell Perkins rejected an author he might regret having missed—William Faulkner. This article is a delightful collection of editors' and publishers' tales that should spur on rejection-shy writers.

Mitgang, Herbert. "How Theodore White Makes a Best-Seller." *New York Times,* July 24, 1982, p. 9.

Spikol, Art. *Magazine Writing: The Inside Angle.* Cincinnati: Writer's Digest Books, 1979.

8

Conclusion: Building on the Skills You Have

It would be dishonest to tell you that writing the last chapter is as difficult as putting together the very first chapter. For me, at least, completing a writing project is still more exciting than any other part of it except the initial planning stages. Once I become immersed in the writing, a momentum grows, a pace that some writers despise and others find the most enticing part of the writing process. "It takes over my life," is the way one nonfiction writer turned novelist describes the later stages of the writing process. However, as I have become more attuned to the *process*, rather than the *product*, of writing, I have become a more contented writer during the in-between stages of research, first draft, revisions, final draft, and critiques with each project. I move closer to enjoying all stages of writing, not just "having written."

By now you are well aware of the improvements effective nonfiction writing can make in your business, professional, or school career. Take a moment to consider some of the personal benefits, beyond the satisfaction offered by letter writing (staying in touch with friends or relatives). In her eye-opening book *Self Therapy: Techniques for Personal Growth* (Berkeley, Calif.: Bookpeople, 1967), therapist and teacher Muriel Schiffman lists writing as one of the three paths to exploring your hidden emotions. (The other two ways are talking and thinking.) Schiffman, whose letters to me over the years have been a source of inspiration and information, explains in *Self Therapy* how to do an "emotional freewrite," as readers of this book will recognize it to be, to get at hidden feeling:

> . . . You must be *in the midst of an emotional experience*. If you sit down to write about a problem in cold blood you may end

137

up with the story of your life, but that is not self therapy. The purpose of self therapy is to feel the emotion you are hiding *right now,* not merely theorize about your past. You must start with an apparent emotion. Write while this cover feeling is hot off the griddle; do not wait till it cools off.

. . . Writing is the quickest way I know to find a hidden feeling. The whole process should not take more than ten to twenty minutes. . . . Write the question, *What am I feeling?* Begin by describing your apparent emotion. . . . *Describe your physical symptoms.* When you are finished, destroy the paper. . . .

I hope this book has inspired you to realize that writing is not a mystical experience but the product of hard work, albeit creative, thoughtful work. I would be pleased to learn that this book has inspired you to write, to write more effectively, or to experience the other benefits of writing. One professor, blocked for several years, credits his return to writing to a freewriting workshop that he attended:

. . . I now know that I can write and that I have some talent to do it. Now I hunger to write, to express, to create meaning through my pen and paper. I have a voice inside of me that is straining to be heard and that won't accept silence any longer. I have a hunger for the recognition and pride that writing will bring me. I find that writing, whatever the form, taps into a part of myself that is hidden from my conscious mind. At times when I write I feel as if I am taken over by an alter ego, that writing opens up a secret gate in my being and lets out a deep part of me that has no other avenue of expression or existence. I love it! I don't think anything could stop me from writing now, except apathy about myself. . . .

I have to correct my associate's overzealousness, however. Writing *may* bring recognition; it may not, or if it does, recognition may be a long time coming. What is clear is that poor writing will certainly bring the kind of recognition we can all do without. Wordiness, shoddy research, clichés, dull sentences, misspellings, run-on sentences—these are examples of bad writing that will harm school papers, personal letters, or business and professional writing tasks—and even reputations.

Here, then, in summary form, are the basic steps to success in nonfiction writing:

1. Come up with an idea, or zero in on an assignment.

2. Do any necessary background research on your topic. Who else has written on this subject? What have they said? What are the controversies in the issue you are writing about? What are the unanswered questions?

3. Do original research, as needed. Who will you inteview? What will you observe? What existing sources will you examine? Should you conduct a survey?

4. Make notes for your final written product throughout the writing process, from inception of the idea through the research, writing, and rewriting stages.

5. Make an outline, or a list of points to cover, to use in organizing your thoughts for your first draft.

6. Write, edit, and rewrite this draft until you are satisfied this is your best effort. (You may have to go back and do more work on any of the previous steps based upon what you have learned—or failed to learn—as reflected in your actual manuscript.)

7. If necessary, check quotations with experts or authorities, verify statistics, facts, or published quotations by comparing to original sources or your notes.

8. Proofread, make any final changes, and retype so your final version is letter perfect and ready for submission.

9. If possible, give your final manuscript to outside readers—colleagues, freelance editors, friends, relatives—before submission.

10. Type a cover letter and send your manuscript along to your editor, or write a memo and send your writing (report, evaluation, etc.) to your employer. (If the manuscript is not an assignment, write and send a query letter with a sample of your completed manuscript on speculation.)

11. If writing for publication, even if you have a firm assignment, keep track of your submissions by noting when and to whom your manuscript or query letter was sent. (Include a post card so you will be assured your manuscript arrived safely.) If you have not had a response after four weeks to two months, write a follow-up letter, or make a phone call, inquiring about the status of your submission. (See sample submission sheet following.)

RECORD OF CIRCULATING MANUSCRIPTS, PROPOSALS, AND QUERIES

Title	Format	Sent to (Place)	Editor
		1. _____	_____
		2. _____	_____
		3. _____	_____
		4. _____	_____
		5. _____	_____
		6. _____	_____
		7. _____	_____
		8. _____	_____
		9. _____	_____
		10. _____	_____
		1. _____	_____
		2. _____	_____
		3. _____	_____
		4. _____	_____
		5. _____	_____
		6. _____	_____
		7. _____	_____
		8. _____	_____
		9. _____	_____
		10. _____	_____

1. __
2. __
3. __
4. __
5. __
6. __
7. __
8. __
9. __
10. __

1. __
2. __
3. __
4. __
5. __
6. __
7. __
8. __
9. __
10. __

RECORD OF CIRCULATING MANUSCRIPTS, PROPOSALS, AND QUERIES

Date Sent	Follow Up	Returned	Published

12. Keep all notes, correspondence, drafts of your manuscript, and material related to the project in a folder. Even after publication, consider storing this information for later use. You may, however, wish to prune your research materials, retaining only primary or secondary research that cannot easily be gathered or located again.

If you are at all serious about nonfiction writing, you should take a few moments to learn the basic proofreading symbols. These symbols simplify communication among writer, editor, and publisher. Anyone who will aid you in retyping your writing, such as a secretary or a typist, should also learn the symbols that follow. If you only write for business purposes, communication about your writing will be facilitated if you use editing/proofreading symbols. Even if you write only for personal reasons, you will find these symbols convenient for any writing situation that requires more than a first draft.

	ℛ delete	ⓣⓡ	transpose
	ℋ paragraph	stet	leave as is
no	ℋ no paragraph	↻	close up space
	⊙ insert period	＃	insert space

Corrections on galleys or proofs for the printer are always done in the margin; you, however, may wish to make corrections on your manuscript directly within the body of your text, noting such insertions with a caret (∧). If the insertion is lengthy, type it on a separate page and show where it is to be added to your text by means of a caret and the word *insert* circled in the margin. Be sure to indicate on your separate sheet the manuscript page where the material should be inserted.

A NONFICTION WRITING PLAN

Whether you are writing for your job, school career, or yourself, to approach writing like a professional means meeting deadlines, creating long-term plans and, within those plans, deciding on short-term priorities. There is no one way to write like a professional. Some writers write when they have a deadline to meet; others keep fixed hours, like bankers. It is safe to say, however, that in the beginning, whether your writing is a memo assigned by your boss, or an article that you want to research and write for possible publication, deadlines you impose on yourself—or that are imposed by others—will help keep you on track.

Conceptualize your writing as two kinds of activities:

1. Writing you *have* to do (assigned work)
2. Writing you *want* to do (for self-expression, job advancement, fun, etc.)

Although failing to do required writing projects may get you fired, or flunked, failing to do the ones you want to do may have even more dire long-term consequences.

Writing takes time, practice, and effort. Your confidence in yourself as a writer will increase as you write and read more. Writing requires thought, to be sure; but getting words down on paper requires sitting down (or standing up, if you prefer) and simply doing it. Therefore, block out hours, days, weeks, or even a set period each year that you will devote to both reactive and active types of writing.

As with any time-management concern, if you do not know where you want to go with your writing, you will not know how to get there. Goals are necessary for your writing. Without them you drift, block, freeze, and react erratically to writing assignments and opportunities. Do you have a grand writing scheme? Setting goals facilitates writing like a professional. What are your long-term writing goals? What are your short-term writing priorities? Set goals for your writing; it will help you in the day-to-day way you manage your writing time. Use the space below to write down important long-term writing goals:

Long-Term Writing Goals

1. _____
2. _____
3. _____

Look over your list and *prioritize* your writing goals. Decide what project you will tackle first. Doing too many projects at once may result in lots of planning and flurries of activity and little finished work. (Remember the example of Brian in Chapter 2, who avoided one writing project by thinking up others.)

Now consider a writing plan that will enable you to achieve your goal, whether that means an article in a national magazine, an annual report that gets you a promotion, or a book that gets you on Johnny Carson's show:

Short-Term Priorities to Achieving My Main Writing Goal

1. _____
2. _____
3. _____
4. _____

Set deadlines for each priority. If attending a writer's conference will help you to achieve your long-term goal, find out which ones are available in your community, and set aside time to attend them. (*Writer's Digest* and *The Writer,* available by subscription or at some newsstands, are monthly magazines that will inform you of such conferences.) Don't put attending a writer's conference, or any other short-term priority, aside for too long, or your writing plans will stay nothing more than dreams.

You may decide that you would benefit from joining groups whose members are full-time or part-time professional writers, or by starting a group of your own. There are numerous groups and resources available to improve and refine your nonfiction writing skills, and to bring you into contact with fellow nonfiction writers. Some of those resources are listed below.

WRITERS' ORGANIZATIONS

All the writing membership organizations listed below have eligibility requirements as well as annual membership dues. Write for a membership packet from those organizations you think you might be qualified for. Almost all have monthly newsletters for members that contain valuable technical and marketing information. Some groups, like the ASJA and IRE, are mostly for nonfiction writers; others, like the Authors Guild and PEN, have members who write fiction and nonfiction, or who write both.

American Society of Journalists and Authors, Inc. (ASJA)
1501 Broadway
Suite 1907
New York, New York 10036
     Nonfiction magazine and book authors. Members also do a variety of related writing, such as brochures, speechwriting, newsletters, annual reports. Sponsors Dial-a-Writer service to link companies and publishers with potential authors. The Annual Writers' Conference is held each spring in New York City.

Authors Guild, Inc.
234 West 44th Street
New York, New York 10036
     Members are nonfiction and fiction book authors. The Guild is active in contract and legal concerns of its members; and it sponsors a symposium on writing issues.

The Drama Desk
41 West 72nd Street
New York, New York 10023
     Members are mostly theater critics.

Investigative Reporters & Editors, Inc. (IRE)
220 Walter Williams Hall
University of Missouri
Columbia, Missouri 65211
     Newspaper journalists and journalism professors comprise their membership. Sponsors an annual conference devoted to reporting techniques and ethical concerns.

The Newspaper Guild (TNG)
1125 15th Street, N.W.
Washington, D.C. 20005
     For reporters who are members of this union.

PEN American Center
47 Fifth Avenue
New York, New York 10013
     Poets, playwrights, and nonfiction and fiction book authors comprise PEN. Publishes an annual guide to grants and prizes

available to writers ($5 including postage). Sponsors numerous readings and literary events in New York City.

Society of Professional Journalists
Sigma Chi Delta
35 East Wacker Drive
Chicago, Illinois 60601

For professional journalists and teachers of journalism including visual and print media.

Consider contacting your professional or alumni organizations to find out whether there is a writing-related task force or committee that you can become active in, and how to communicate with other professionals or graduates who share your interest in writing. Some professional organizations, like the American Sociology Association, sponsor writing seminars and workshops for those members who wish to improve their writing skills. Other professional organizations publish journals that may occasionally deal with the topic of professional writing. Nurses who want to write, for example, would find a good place to start in Edith P. Lewis's targeted article, "For the Nurse Writer's Bookshelf," an article with a resource listing that appeared in the July 1982 *American Journal of Nursing.*

You might also decide to start your own nonfiction writer's resource or support group. Over the years I have participated in, or started, various nonfiction-writing support/resource groups. My most recent group began in May 1983; it now has twelve participating nonfiction writers or would-be writers. Half the writers are full-time professionals; the others have full-time jobs and have written, or would like to write, or go back to writing, in their spare time. Jamie Raab, a writer and an editor at *Family Circle* magazine, and I each asked a few other writers that we knew to take part in this group, and by the second meeting other writers were calling and asking if they could be included. We meet once a month for an hour and a half. After trying various meeting times, we have discovered that 6–7:30 P.M. on a weekday night is best. It is short, and early enough that social or family evening obligations can still be met. We divide the hour and a half into two segments. One segment gives each writer a chance to use the group—to air gripes, ask for suggestions or feedback, or even talk about writer's block. The other segment is devoted to a theme decided upon by the group one or more months before. One month the second part of the group was devoted to brainstorming about organizing files and research; other months the topics were maintaining contact with editors, travel writing, and book packagers. Some of the meetings include an invited guest speaker.

Before my concluding remarks on nonfiction writing, here are some additional facts about legal considerations, if you intend to publish your writing, as well as how to avoid libeling, invading privacy, or plagiarizing others in your own work.

LEGAL CONSIDERATIONS IF YOU PLAN TO PUBLISH

If you are concerned with copyrighting your own writing, consult such guides as William S. Strong's *The Copyright Book*, Tad Crawford's *The Writer's Legal Guide*, or contact the Copyright Office, Library of Congress, Washington, D.C. 20559 for a free information kit. You can also contact a lawyer, your publisher, or any of the professional writers organizations listed on pages 145–146. This section focuses on procedures you might need to follow in conducting research for nonfiction writing you intend to publish in order to avoid possible lawsuits charging that you violated someone else's copyright, libeled someone, or invaded their privacy.

Releases for Interviews

You generally will not need a written release for using an interview in a published work if you tell your interviewee right up front what you are doing, the use you plan to make of the interview, and if no restrictions are then placed on your use of that material. However, if your interview deals with controversial or intimate material, or if you want to be cautious, you should get a signed release to avoid legal problems later on.

There are all kinds of releases, some more formal than others, and there is no magic formula for requesting a release. For in-person interviews, it is more convenient for you to bring the release with you to the interview and have it signed on the spot. Use your judgment as to whether you should request your interviewee's signature before or after the interview. By asking for a signed release before the interview, you avoid doing an interview that you might be unable to use because permission is subsequently denied. However, you might have gained enough rapport during the interview that a request after the interview will meet with approval in a case where it might not have if requested beforehand. If your interviewee requires approval of what you write, you may have to send him or her a release after you have read the material over the phone, or along with a copy of relevant manuscript pages. Some writers are especially sensitive about allowing anyone to edit their material, particularly interviewees. Often, however, interviewees only want to check for accuracy, or to correct awkward sentences that sounded better than they read.

A sample release for interview material and photographs follows. You should, however, tailor your releases to each writing project as well as with regard to any legal counsel your employer or publisher provides for you.

PHOTOGRAPHS AND PRIVATE FACTS INTERVIEW RELEASE

For and in consideration of my engagement by Arco Publishing, Inc., I agree to the reproduction and sale of interviews I have given _____ and/or of photographs of me, in connection with the book tentatively entitled

_____

and works adapted from this book. My agreement extends to uses in all media, including in advertising and promotional material for this book and works adapted from it.

I understand that because people will be relying on this permission, I will not cancel or revoke it.

I release _____ and Arco Publishing, Inc., as well as people affili-
ated with Arco, and any entity that
obtains rights to

_____

from them, or who reproduces or uses the
interviews and/or photographs in connection with the promotion or sale of this
book or works adapted from it, from any
liability for violation of any right I may
have in connection with those materials,
including rights related to defamation,
privacy, or copyright.

I waive any right to inspect or to approve
the photographs or written material based
on the interviews.

I am ( ) over ( )under the age of eighteen
(18) years.

Witness: Signed:

_____   _____

Dated_____

As guardian of the above-named minor, who
has signed this consent on his or her own
behalf, I approve and ratify the execution
of this release on behalf of that minor.

Dated_____   _____

Permissions for Quoted Material

There are some instances when it is unnecessary to secure
permission to quote or closely paraphrase published material.
Permission need not be secured if the material is in the public
domain, or if you are making "fair use" of it within the meaning
of the copyright definition. A work can fall into the public do-

main for a number of reasons: (1) copyright protection has expired; (2) copyright was never secured; (3) the work has fallen out of copyright because of a technical failure; and (4) it is a United States Government publication.

"Fair use" is a vaguer concept: The law does not set specific limits on the number of words you can use from a published work. Rule of thumb varies, depending on the conservatism of the legal advice. Some interpret "fair use" to mean that you can quote up to two hundred and fifty words from a standard-length book, or up to 10 percent of an article (such as one hundred words of a one-thousand-word newspaper story), and no more than a line from a poem or song lyrics.

If you think you are taking enough written material from any work that permission should be secured, or if you are doubtful and want to cover yourself, you might write to the copyright owner and request a permission. When permissions are involved, there is a wide range of possible outcomes to your request. Results will depend upon the use you plan to make of the reprinted material (for educational, noncommercial versus profit-making publishing concerns) as well as how much you are reprinting (five hundred words or an entire chapter), the kind of material you are reprinting (rules are much stricter for songs, for example, than for prose), as well as luck, greed, whether your work is critical of theirs, or even whether you use language that they find objectionable. You may not be asked to pay anything and may have limitless nonexclusive use of the materials; you may be asked to pay a one-time fee (payable upon publication of your work) of as little as ten dollars or as much as several thousand dollars; or you may be asked to pay a fee upon publication plus royalties based on a fixed or variable percentage of your income from the written property. You may also be denied permission without any reason being given. If permission is denied, you should consider cutting the length of the quoted material so that it falls in the fair use category. Depending upon how important this material is to your writing, you might consult a lawyer to see if you really need to secure permission. This preventive measure may save you time, money, and aggravation in the long run, since once permission has been denied in writing, you may be on shakier ground than if you had done your homework, decided permission was not really necessary, and never asked for it in the first place.

To facilitate obtaining written permission to quote copyrighted material in your own writing, send along a permissions form. (However, if you are dealing with a publisher, they will probably send back their own form.) A sample form follows.

```
SAMPLE PERMISSIONS FORM

Author's (Your) Address
Date
Name of Company, Publisher, Individual
Address
Attn: Copyright/Permissions Department
(for companies)

Dear---:

   I am preparing a book tentatively
entitled ___, to be published about ___ by
___. The book will be published in a
limited hardcover edition for libraries
and a paper edition.
   I would like permission to include in my
book and in future editions thereof,
including nonexclusive world rights in all
languages, [the attached quotations] [the
following photographs] from your [name of
book or other publications] [edition,
volume, page number, date, author, title,
etc].
[leave some space here if you need several
permissions from the same publication,
company, etc.]
[attach ms. page with quote or describe
photograph or drawing]
   These rights will in no way restrict
republication of your material in any form
by you or by others authorized by you.
   For your convenience a release form is
```

provided below and a copy of this letter
is enclosed for your files.
   Thank you for your cooperation.

                 Sincerely yours,

                 Author's Name [you]

encl.

I (we) grant permission for the use requested above.

Date _____   _____
Any special credit line: _____

Libel and Invasion of Privacy

Libel is defined by *Black's Law Dictionary* as "to defame or injure a person's reputation by a published writing." Someone might sue you for libel if you write that he or she committed a crime, was sexually deviant, had a loathsome disease, or was professionally incompetent. You can libel a living person, a corporation, or an organization.

By contrast, you can invade the privacy only of a living person. Invasion of privacy means revealing embarrassing private facts, even if true, or putting someone in a false light. In one case, for example, a biographer wrote that a sports figure had received a bronze star during the Second World War. The sports figure sued the biographer and her publisher, saying that he was caused mental distress because his war buddies thought he had misrepresented himself as having received a medal he had not in fact been awarded. Privacy laws differ from state to state; depending on the particular statement, libel and privacy may be similar. You cannot libel or invade the privacy of dead persons.

Even novelists are not immune from successful libel suits, as was brought home all too clearly by a case in the late 1970s, in which a novelist and her publisher lost a suit brought by a man who said he was the recognizable model for a character in the author's novel. It is more difficult for public figures or public officials to win libel or privacy suits. Due to a Supreme Court ruling that "debate on public issues should be uninhibited, robust and wide open," it seems that public officials and public figures are less protected by libel laws than the average person. It is sometimes, however, difficult to determine just who is a public figure, as lawyer-author Carol E. Rinzler points out in her article, "Who Is That Public Figure—And Why Can You Say All Those Terrible Things About Him?" (*Publishers Weekly,* June 24, 1983).

You cannot prevent someone accusing you of libel or invasion of privacy, but you *can* reduce the risk of the plaintiff's prevailing if such accusations occur. Be certain that you have reliable sources and documentation to substantiate your critical statements. In his booklet *Synopsis of the Law of Libel and the Right of Privacy* (New York: Newspaper Enterprise Association, 1980), attorney Bruce W. Sanford gives ten guidelines for reporters, extracted below, that all nonfiction writers should keep in mind:

1. Avoid slipshod, indifferent, or careless reporting. . . .
2. Truth is a defense, but there may be a vast difference between what's true and what can be proven to be true to a jury. . . .
3. There's no such thing as a "false opinion," so you have greater leeway with expressions of opinion than statements of fact. . . .
4. Watch out for the "routine" story of minor significance. . . . Make reports of arrests, investigations and other judicial or legislative proceedings and records precisely accurate.
5. Try to get "the other side of the story. . . ."
6. Take particular care with quotations. . . .
7. Never railroad a story through, but instead edit it carefully to make sure it says precisely what you want it to say. . . .
8. Avoid borderline cases of invasion of privacy, since the law of the right of privacy is still developing. . . .
9. Don't make unauthorized use of names and pictures for advertising or other commercial purposes. . . .
10. If an error has been made, always handle demands for retractions which come from a lawyer for a potential

plaintiff with the advice of legal counsel. A well-meaning but unnecessary or poorly worded correction may actually prejudice a publisher's or broadcaster's defenses in a subsequent lawsuit.

Plagiarism

Plagiarism is primarily an ethical issue, since most litigation in this area is over copyright infringement. However, plagiarism is an important issue for writers to consider. When I was in public school, there was a joke that "plagiarism" was using one source and "research" was using three or more. I recently got a phone call from a distraught friend who is a successful corporate executive. It seemed his thesis adviser had plagiarized part of my friend's own writing. "Right there, in the middle of his manuscript, were two pages copied word for word from my thesis," my friend screamed. "There was no footnote. My thesis wasn't even mentioned in his bibliography!"

The anger my friend expressed at seeing his writing pirated after he had worked so hard on it is not uncommon in cases of plagiarism. Plagiarism is a serious offense, defined in *Black's Law Dictionary*, 5th ed., (St. Paul, Minn.: West Publishing Co., 1971), as "The act of appropriating the literary composition of another, or parts or passages of his writings, or the ideas and language of the same, and passing them off as the product of one's own mind." Authors should, of course, make every effort to avoid plagiarism.

If you quote from another writer *or* use another's ideas or language even in part, be sure to acknowledge your indebtedness by citing the published or unpublished source of what you've borrowed. Be sure to handle borrowed material carefully: Quotations must be exact, and the author's work must not be misrepresented (for example, by changing the tone or implications of the context in which the borrowed material appears). If you paraphrase, choose your own words carefully and be very sure to represent the original author's work accurately. Paraphrased material should be used to support your own ideas and arguments rather than to substitute for them. It is important that you realize that paraphrasing rather than quoting does not relieve you of the responsibility of acknowledging your source.

If footnotes are not used for either stylistic or cost reasons, consider other options that will still give definite credit to the source of your material. For example, you might mention the author by name, including a more complete citation in your bibliography, or you might include a complete or abbreviated citation right in your text.

Put yourself in the other author's position. How would you feel if you saw that little or that much of your work unacknowledged in someone else's work? Are you copying or paraphrasing and giving ample credit to the source, in the text, in the footnotes, on the copyright page or in the bibliography, so that the first author gets some credit and exposure (if not direct income) from your use of that material? Is your use of that research fair or abusive? If you met that author in person and you learned she read your report or published work, would you smile and feel completely comfortable, or would you slink down, feeling like a thief?

And so, dear reader, the text of *How to Write Like a Professional* comes to an end. I have been challenged, frustrated, and gratified by this chance to share with you what I have learned about nonfiction writing during my professional career. Here are my last thoughts on writing before I lead you to the exercises and references in this chapter: Be critical of your own writing. Strive to improve what you say on paper, but avoid being so overcritical that you completely freeze or live in fear of the outer critics. It is true that if you have not written it, no one will read what you had hoped to say; each writing task presents another opportunity for improvement and to get closer to writing with joy and confidence, not agony.

EXERCISES

1. Look over the nonfiction writing journal that you are keeping. Rewrite any exercises of particular use to you. Continue your nonfiction writing journal even after your finish this book.

2. As a final writing exercise, and to give me valuable feedback about the strengths and weaknesses of *How to*

Write Like a Professional, consider writing a memo, letter, or review of this book and sending it to me at the following address:

J.L. Barkas, Ph.D.
P.O. Box 31
Cooper Station
New York, New York 10276

I cannot absolutely promise you a reply, but I will certainly read and think about any materials that you send to me.

ADDITIONAL REFERENCES

Adams, W. Royce. *Think, Read, React, Plan, Write, Rewrite,* 3rd ed. New York: Holt, Rinehart and Winston, 1982.

American Society of Journalists and Authors. *The Complete Guide to Writing Nonfiction,* edited by Glen Evans. Cincinnati: Writer's Digest Books, 1983. Some 108 professional writers share their expertise on nonfiction writing with an emphasis on specialization: basics of nonfiction writing, as well as how to find, and write for, markets are also included.

Anderson, David, and Peter Benjaminson. *Investigative Reporting.* Bloomington, Indiana: Indiana University Press, 1976. The authors, reporters for the *Detroit Free Press,* spell out techniques for researching and writing a story and getting it published.

Coser, Lewis A., Charles Kadushin, and Walter W. Powell. *Books: The Culture & Commerce of Publishing.* New York: Basic Books, Inc., 1982. Three sociologists teamed up to conduct original research and interpret their findings on the question, "Who decides what America reads?"

Crawford, Tad. *The Writer's Legal Guide.* New York: Hawthorn Books, Inc., 1977.

Goldfarb, Ronald L. and James C. Raymond. *Clear Understandings: A Guide to Legal Writing.* New York: Random House, 1982. Although geared to practicing attorneys, chapters on style, punctuation, and organization will be beneficial to most nonfiction writers.

Kindilien, Carlin. *Basic Writing Skills.* New York: Arco Publishing, Inc., 1982. A simple guide to the content and style of expository writing.

Rico, Gabriele Lusser. *Writing the Natural Way.* Los Angeles: J.P. Tarcher, Inc., 1983. A variation on freewriting and free association to develop natural writing abilities.

Strong, William S. *The Copyright Book: A Practical Guide.* Cambridge, Mass.: The MIT Press, 1981.

Writer's Digest. *Writer's Digest Diary.* Cincinnati: Writer's Digest Books, issued annually in August. A useful blank diary for recording your daily writing-related activities, ideas, and appointments.

Index

Acceptance, 105–106, 109, 111, 112, 113, 134
Agent, 104–105, 113, 118
American Society of Journalists and Authors (ASJA), 10, 109, 144–145, 156
Appropriateness, 83, 100
Article. *See* Journals, Magazines, or Newspapers.
Ashbell, Bernard, 24
Asimov, Isaac, 9
Assignments, 1, 46, 112, 139, 143
Audience, 3, 7, 8, 10, 19, 32, 45, 66, 81–82, 83, 87, 96–98, 99, 104–105, 111, 115, 120
Authors Guild, 144–145

Baker, Russell, 9
Barzun, Jacques, 37, 50, 66
Bibliographic card, 64–65, 79
Bibliographic style, 78, 99
Book proposal, 107, 108, 119–128, 131
Book publishers, 117–120, 128
Book reviews, 115–116, 156
Book writing schedule, 128–132
Books, 4, 13, 17, 22, 25, 37–38, 46, 47, 48, 49, 84, 104, 106, 119, 120, 134, 144, 156
Burnout, 14, 22

Capote, Truman 17
Clarity, 7, 8, 78–83, 99, 100
Conferences, 8, 109, 144
Content, 1, 3, 8, 45–67, 100, 116
Copyright, 147, 150, 154–155, 157
Correctness. *See* Grammar.
Correspondence. *See* Letters.
Criticism, 4–5, 7, 8–9, 14–15, 19–20, 25–26, 129, 137, 139, 155
    fear of, 19–20

Deadlines, 9, 11, 12, 14, 21, 24–26, 28, 66, 98, 112, 128, 142–143, 144
Denenberg, R. V., 34
Dial-a-Writer, 145
Diamond, Lynn, 25
Dickens, Charles, 74
Didion, Joan, 9, 50
Dissertations, 12, 13, 98–100, 101, 102
Drafts, 2, 27, 32, 35, 82, 84, 98, 137, 139, 142. *See also* First draft or Last draft.

Editing, 3, 16, 17, 28, 32, 117, 139, 148

Editor, 1, 11, 27, 103, 105, 107–109, 110, 111, 112, 113, 115, 116–117, 119, 120, 131–134, 142

Elbow, Peter, *Writing With Power*, 10, 24, 25

Elements of Style. See William Strunk, Jr.

Emerson, Ralph Waldo, 49, 66

Exams, 2, 5, 98–99

Existing sources, 51, 62–65, 128, 139

Expository writing. *See* Nonfiction writing.

"Fair use," 149–150

Feedback. *See* Criticism.

Feierman, Joanne, 70, 71

Fetherston, Drew, 18, 40

Fielden, John S., 46, 79–80, 83–84

Final draft. *See* Last draft.

Finkelstein, Carol Ann, 19

First draft, 4, 17, 22, 23, 24, 27, 32, 36, 80, 81–82, 92, 98, 105, 112, 129, 137

Flesch, Rudolf, 7, 10, 78

Footnotes, 99, 115, 155

Freewrite, 10, 24, 27, 28, 50, 82, 85, 137–138

Gathering information. *See* Research

Getting published, 8, 10, 103–136

Gorden, Raymond L., 52

Grammar, 37, 69, 75–78, 99, 117

Ideas, 2, 3, 4, 6, 13, 15, 16, 17, 19, 20, 45, 46–50, 99, 103, 106, 109, 112, 114, 120, 134, 139

International Directory of Little Magazines and Small Presses, 114

interviews, 50, 51, 52–58, 66, 80, 110, 128, 139, 147–149

releases for, 147–149

invasion of privacy, 147, 152–154

IRE (Investigative Reporters & Editors), 144–145

Irwin, Theodore, 3

jargon, 78–97, 85

Jong, Erica, 9

journals, 7, 8, 37, 38, 46, 104, 114–116

Kaiser, Charles, 6

karate-chop method, 25

"kill fee," 113

Lambuth, David, *The Golden Book of Writing*, 69, 77

Lasch, Christopher, 69

Last draft, 23, 31, 89, 129, 132

Legal considerations in writing, 147–155

Letters, 6, 25, 32, 35, 46, 47, 49, 83, 87, 88–93, 100–101, 137, 155

Business, 90–93, 116

Personal, 32, 89–90, 137, 138

Query, 106–110, 112, 113, 114, 115, 116, 119, 120, 134, 139

to the editor, 111

Libel, 147, 152–154

Library, 18, 31, 37–38, 41, 62–63, 100, 119

LMP/Literary Market Place, 114, 118

Mack, Karin, *Overcoming Writing Blocks*, 11, 29
Magazines, 1, 4, 8, 37, 46, 48, 62–63, 104, 107, 110, 111–114, 144
Manuscript, 104, 110, 139, 142
    Format for, 114–117
    Unsolicited, 104
Mayer, Martin, 9
McWilliams, Peter, 35–63, 42
Meditation, 26
Memo, 1, 4, 6, 12, 25, 45, 46, 49, 71, 83, 87, 93–95, 101, 139, 143, 156
Michener, James, 9
Moran, Terence, 2
ms. See Manuscript.
Multiple submissions, 116

Newspapers, 8, 15, 48, 62–63, 104, 106, 107, 110–113
Nonfiction writing. *See also* Writing.
    Self-expression, 1, 137–138, 143
    Basic steps, 3, 4, 117, 138–139
    Book writing schedule, 128–132
    Journal, 6, 9, 28, 37, 60, 155
    Legal considerations, 147–155
    Library for, 37
    Organizations, 8, 144–147
    Plan, 8, 9, 89, 142–144
    Schedule, 9–10, 21, 28–29
    Survey, 1, 13–15, 23
    Teaching of, 1, 2, 5, 10, 69–72, 86
Notetaking, 55, 56, 63–65, 79, 139

Observations, 51, 58–60, 128, 139
Olds, Sally Wendkos, 73–74
Organization. *See* Outline or Organizing principles.
Organizing material, 3, 4, 46, 50, 77, 79–82, 84, 99, 156
Organizing principles, 80–82, 85, 97–98
Orwell, George, 58–59
Outline, 7, 8, 13, 22, 25, 79–80, 118, 119–120, 134, 139

Pannell Kerr Forster. *See* Charles Kaiser.
PEN, 144–146
Perfectionism, 16–17
Permissions, 117, 129, 131, 149–152
    Sample form, 151–152
Photocopying, 33
Plagiarism, 154–155
Process of writing, 2, 5, 17, 18, 23, 26, 41, 80, 137
Procrastination, 11–12, 20, 28, 29
Proofreading, 117, 139, 142
Prose. *See* Nonfiction writing.
Public domain, 149–150
Punctuation, 8, 26, 45, 69, 75–76, 77, 84, 99, 156

Query letter, 106–110, 112, 113, 114, 115, 116, 119, 120, 134, 139
Questionnaires, 60–61

Radovsky, Saul S., 74
Readability. *See* Clarity or Style.
Reader appeal. *See* Appropriateness.
Reading, 4, 6, 7, 8, 18, 23, 26, 28, 51, 143

References. *See* Resources.
Rejection, 105–106, 109, 110, 112, 134, 135
Reliability. *See* Content.
Report, 1, 2, 4, 6, 45, 46, 47, 81, 83, 87, 95–98, 101, 144
Research, 3, 4, 6, 13, 17–18, 20, 23, 25, 35, 38, 45, 50–67, 80, 99, 105, 118, 128, 138, 139, 142
    Limitations on, 51
Resources, 8, 31
Retyping, 31, 34, 35, 82, 108, 117, 139
Revision. *See* Rewriting and Editing.
Reward system, 21, 25, 28
Rewriting, 1, 3, 4, 5, 10, 16, 17, 28, 32, 50, 80, 85, 96, 101, 117, 129, 137, 139, 155
Roueche, Berton, 9

Safan-Gerard, Desy, 16, 17, 29
Safran, Claire, 31–32
Self-confidence about writing, 3, 7, 8, 14, 23, 27, 75, 143
"Selling block," 134
Silden, Isobel, 26
Singer, Isaac Bashevis, 32
Skjei, Eric, *Overcoming Writing Blocks*, 11, 29
Society of Magazine Writers. *See American Society of Journalists and Authors.*
Speculation, 109, 110, 113, 115, 139
Speaking, 1, 8, 10, 19, 51, 70, 87–88
Speech, 1, 49, 119
Spelling, 7, 8, 35, 70, 75, 77, 99, 116, 117, 138
Strunk, William Jr., and White, E. B., *Elements of Style*, 10, 37, 77, 86

Style, 1, 3, 7, 8, 10, 45, 69–86, 100, 116, 156
Style sheet, 77–78, 105
Submissions
    Format, 114–117
    Multiple, 116
Surveys. *See* Questionnaires.

Tape recorder, 26–27, 33, 37, 41, 55, 56
Tarshis, Barry, 70–71
Term paper, 1, 98–99, 138
Thesis, 98–100
Thoreau, Henry David, 72
Thought. *See* Content.
Time management, 23, 38, 42, 98, 99, 128, 143
Todd, Alden, *Finding Facts Fast*, 62
Toffler, Alvin, 9
Tools. *See* Writing Tools.
Tuchman, Gail Schiller, 40–41
Turabian, Kate L., 99, 102
Turkel, Studs, 9
Typewriter, 31–33, 34, 36, 37, 38, 39, 41, 80
Typing, 31, 116

Unsolicited manuscript, 104

Vegetarianism, 108, 119

White, E.B. *See* Strunk, William J.
Wolfe, Thomas, 22, 38
Word processor, 31–32, 33, 34–36, 80, 82, 108, 116
Writer's block, 5, 8, 11–29, 39, 41, 80, 98, 99, 100, 128, 134, 147
    Causes, 15–22, 29, 143
    Manifestations of, 13–14
    Solutions, 23–29, 39

Writer's Market, 114
Writing. *See also* Nonfiction writing.
    Conferences, 8, 109, 144
    Organizations, 144–147
    Place, 18–19, 38–41
    Plan, 8, 9, 89, 142–144

Writing (*continued*)
    Tools, 8, 31–43; List of, 36–37
    Traveling kit, 41
    Workshops, 5, 146

Zinsser, William, *On Writing Well,* 3, 10, 79, 86